WHAT ABOUT NOUTHETIC COUNSELING?

**A Question and Answer Book
with
History, Help and Hope
for the Christian Counselor**

By Jay E. Adams

PRESBYTERIAN AND REFORMED PUBLISHING CO.
Phillipsburg, New Jersey
1980

ISBN: 0-87552-064-2

PRINTED IN THE UNITED STATES OF AMERICA

CONTENTS

Preface v
Chapters
  I - Part One
    A Quick Look At Nouthetic Counseling 1
  II - Part One
    Counseling And The Sovereignty of God 7
    Part Two
    Do You Really Believe That? 21
    Questions:
      1. Do you think that feelings are unimportant? 22
      2. Why don't you say more about empathy? 24
      3. Don't you believe in any kind of mental illness? 26
      4. Do you believe that all of our problems are due to sin? 28
      5. Don't you think that we can learn something from
         psychologists? 29
      6. What do you mean by confrontation? 30
      7. Why are you so critical of the views of others? 31
      8. Are you sure that Freud, Rogers, Skinner, et al are
         competing with the pastor and trying to carry on activities
         that overlap and usurp his? 33
      9. Why don't you write more fully about the counselor as a
         godly man? 36
     10. Why don't you engage in dialogue with Christian
         psychologists and psychiatrists? 39
     11. Can a pastor do all of the counseling that you seem to
         think needs to be done in a local church? Will a pastor
         have time to do it? 40
     12. How does your approach differ from Job's comforters'
         approach? 41
     13. What about love in your counseling? 43
     14. What do you do when someone feels inferior? 46

iii

15. Why don't you ever speak about people's problems in terms of game theory as many other counselors do?.. 48

16. Why do you use a desk in counseling? 50

17. You say a lot about the possible significance of sleep loss. Suppose sleep loss is important. What do I do to get to sleep when I find myself having difficulty doing so? .. 51

18. What does the word nouthetic mean? 53

19. How do you counsel unsaved persons? 54

20. How long does it take to become an effective nouthetic counselor? 57

21. Have you done research on the results of nouthetic counseling? 58

22. Why can't you use the methods of other counseling systems? 59

23. What is conscience? 62

24. How is it in the history of the world that we are just now discovering all about nouthetic counseling? 63

25. How do you counsel husbands and wives when only one will come?...................................... 64

Part Three

Your Relationship To Nouthetic Counseling 70

PREFACE

It is time for this book. To take stock, to straighten out misunderstandings and to look forward to the future is an important task for any person who has been closely involved with a movement for some time. By doing so, he can gain perspective. Hopefully this assessment after ten years of nouthetic counseling will be helpful to others as well.

Jay E. Adams, 1976
dean, The Institute of Pastoral Studies
of the Christian Counseling and Educational Foundation
and
Visiting Professor of Practical Theology at
Westminster Theological Seminary

CHAPTER ONE
PART ONE

A QUICK LOOK AT NOUTHETIC COUNSELING

Nouthetic counseling has been growing rapidly.[1] I prefer the words "biblical" or "Christian" but reluctantly I have used the word nouthetic in the title and throughout the text of this book simply as a convenience by which the biblical system of counseling that has been developed in such books as *Competent to Counsel* and *The Christian Counselor's Manual* might be identified most easily.[2] This phenomenal growth among pastors, elders and other leaders in the evangelical church has occasioned a good bit of discussion; some negative; most positive. As a result, scores of book reviews, magazine articles, numerous analyses, classroom studies, two masters theses and one doctoral dissertation have been forthcoming.[3]

A number of seminaries, colleges and Bible schools are now teaching the principles of nouthetic counseling and using the basic texts in which it is set forth. But as the result of this discussion and interest, all sorts of notions and concepts purporting to be nouthetic

---

[1]The word nouthetic is pronounced *nouthetic,* (as in new) not *nowthetic* (as I have heard some pronouncing it).

[2]The reason why the title Nouthetic Confrontation is not to be preferred is because while admirably embracing the major biblical concepts of counseling, the use of *nouthesia* is not universal. It appears almost exclusively in Paul. Other terms are employed by other writers. For instance, *"paracletic help"* might have been used if John's vocabulary were more prominent in those passages having to do with counseling.

[3]Six formal lectureships have resulted in addition to scores of one or more day conferences in educational institutions. Interest is now worldwide. The writer has just returned from a lecture tour in Germany and Switzerland, and at present has accepted invitations to speak in Hawaii, Ireland, Mexico, Brazil and Columbia.

principles have been spread abroad, some of which are totally erroneous, others true so far as they go but deficient in one or more particulars, and still others true enough but badly stated — usually because they place undue emphasis upon certain matters, that for one reason or other intrigue the commentator, while underplaying others.

Moreover, all sorts of persons today are doing what they call nouthetic counseling. One counselor whom I have never met has a sign hanging outside reading "Nouthetic Counseling." Another has on his stationery "Nouthetic Counselor." Neither man has been trained at our center. While I can only rejoice at the efforts of such persons, I must caution the reader that there is reason to believe that some of what is being done ought to be differentiated from true nouthetic counseling in name since in practice there is little that resembles it. I do not say that all of the misrepresentations are deliberate; nor that all are bad. (I can and do continually learn from others who study and apply God's Word.) And, indeed, perhaps I am to blame for some of the misunderstandings. I do not think that I have been unclear, but I may have been spotty in my treatments of certain subjects, and I am surely deficient at many points. Yet, let me warn that everything purporting to be nouthetic is not necessarily so.

I do, however, want to take a moment to say something more about clarity. I always have sought to speak and write clearly. I have spent years studying the principles of good communication, and I am convinced that clarity is one of the fundamentals to be desired. I believe that all truth, no matter how difficult it may be, can be communicated in an intelligible and interesting manner. I have worked hard at this (certainly not always succeeding). Moreover, since my efforts to help others have focused not merely upon the *what to* but also (practically) upon the *how to,* I have labored to demonstrate how abstract principles can be turned into concrete action, and how general truths may be fleshed out by specific Christian living. For these reasons at times I have been charged with being simplistic. I do not think that this charge has been substantiated. The work that I have done may not always show on the surface, but behind it lies a lifetime of strenuous exegesis and theological reflection. Simple language no more indicates simplistic thinking than complex language indicates profundity of thought.

Moreover, the reader always should bear in mind that sin complicates; righteousness simplifies. The Watergate cover-up amply illustrates the fact.

My efforts for clarity have (to my surprise) made my writings available to all; not merely to professionals or specialists. That has caused a considerable amount of concern (or joy, depending on how one views it from his own standpoint). As a result the counseling caste system is beginning to break down in Christian circles. Christians everywhere are finding that God enables them and expects them to counsel someone, someway.[4] Pastors in particular are coming back into their own as healers of the flock, and (in general) there has been more genuine interest and concern about counseling than we have seen at any previous period in American Church history. That can be good (or bad) according to whether this interest centers upon counseling as an *end in itself* or as a means by which members of the church can be freed to do the work to which God has called them.[5]

Clarity also has earned for me a dubious reputation for "brashness," for "telling it as it is," and for "laying it on the line." Some who consider this a fault should be more cautious in the ways that they simplistically misrepresent my views by failing to take note of the careful qualifications that I have labored to make both in the text (look for words like "largely, partly, ordinarily," etc.) and in various footnotes of my books (where I often qualify more fully). I cannot accept blame for superficiality where the charge actually grows out of superficiality on the part of the reader.

All that I have said thus far should make it perfectly evident (even to such readers) that I consider both clarity and simplicity virtues, not vices. In my opinion, whatever darkens understanding is a detriment; whatever lightens it deserves praise. That I shall attempt to be more and more clear in all that I write should be plain from the fact that my desire to write this book was motivated by that very

---

[4]For more information on this, see my article "You Are Your Brother's Counselor" in *The Big Umbrella:* Presbyterian and Reformed Pub. Co., Nutley, 1973.

[5]For a fuller understanding of my views on this (especially in relationship to evangelism), read Jay Adams, *Your Place In the Counseling Revolution:* Presbyterian and Reformed Pub. Co., Nutley, 1975.

purpose. I look on clarity as a sacred obligation of a Christian minister, whether he speaks from the pulpit or whether he writes with his pen. Obscurity is the father of heresy and ambiguity is the mother of all error. Clarity bears a close relationship to truth.

Nouthetic counseling did not spring from my head, full blown; there has been continued growth in understanding and some significant filling out as well as systematization of both the theory and practice over the last nine years.[6] That growth continues. Although I am thankful that I have found it unnecessary to withdraw or change in any significant way what I wrote in my first published book on counseling *(Competent to Counsel),* I cheerfully admit that it was not the last word! My efforts to update and to supplement by the regular publication of new and additional materials give evidence to my understanding of this fact. I have sought to keep the counselor aware of all new insights as soon as they were adequately thought through, tested by use and could be made available. Subsequent study, although remarkably confirming all of the basic thrusts of *Competent,* nevertheless, has expanded some of them considerably.[7]

---

[6]For instance, in *Competent to Counsel* I did not handle the problem of fear. That was because at that time I did not have adequate answers to some of the problems connected with the subject. The biblical insights connected with the put off-put on dynamic for change also were later coming. The *Manual,* then, offers an advance upon *Competent,* and should be viewed in this way. At the moment, I am working on a number of other issues not heretofore presented in any of the books.

[7]Indeed, slight modifications have been made. For instance, guilt once was considered to be *the* underlying cause in depression. Now, while continuing to recognize guilt as a significant factor in depression, I have come to see that in many cases it may be secondary (guilt arising from following feelings and thus leading to failure to fulfill one's obligations and responsibilities). The original *down* feeling (we all get down from time to time) may not always be occasioned by sin leading to guilt (cf. II Cor. 4:8), but also from legitimate causes. Depression, however, results from handling a down period wrongly, by following feelings rather than following responsibilities. Then guilt arises. Any number of causes of down periods may be isolated: sin, sickness, business or social reverses, etc. But like Paul (in the passage just cited) one who is *down* need not be *down and out.* Depression is a state in which one no longer functions as he should. This movement from *down* (not depression) to *down and out* (depression) occurs whenever one handles down feelings sinfully (thus incurring guilt and more guilt feelings), by following them rather than his responsibilities before God. All this I have made clear in my fuller expositions of depression in the *Manual* and in the pamphlet on depression in the *What Do You Do When* series.

So, at this ten year juncture, it seemed in order to make an assessment and out of that to issue a statement of where things are, where they seem to be heading, and why. I sincerely hope that this statement likewise will clear up a number of the misconceptions that are becoming more or less standard in certain circles because of unfriendly and usually simplistic misinterpretations, or simply out of general confusion.

Other objectives also are in view as I write. Among them let me mention two. Perhaps the second section of this book (Part Two), among other things could be used as something of a primer to introduce students to *some* (I emphasize that word because by no means is it intended to be systematic or complete) of the basic principles of biblical counseling. Secondly, Parts One and Three, in which I have attempted to share something of the past and present goals and visions of the movement, may help others who have not been so directly associated with the work of counseling to understand what some of the discussion is all about. In this way it may be possible for them more intelligently to take a stand for or against nouthetic counseling. Yet, I do hope that their judgments will be made only after reading at least *Competent to Counsel,* the *Manual* and *The Use of the Scriptures in Counseling.* This book alone is incomplete.

Because the first phase of this movement has been so closely associated with my writing, teaching, and speaking I have referred to what has happened almost biographically. I regret the need to do so, yet there was hardly any other way to go. But fortunately, in His providence, as I write, the second phase not only has begun but now is in full swing. If God gives me the occasion, the inclination, and the opportunity, in another ten years I shall report again, but I am convinced that most of what I shall write then will be in the third person.

If God has used me, it is as a pioneer. Much of what I am doing (I know) is outhouse work (there is little indoor plumbing). The territory was virgin; I have learned to use the axe and the machete to clear the trees and the underbrush. The structures I have erected are built solidly, I trust, and should last. But much work needs to be done — much more than I can do alone. God has raised up others who are now at work. Superb young men, beginning where I have come only by my middle years, are fully aware of these needs and now are hard at work making the adjustments, putting in the bathrooms, laying tile, etc. Over the next ten years (and beyond) you should hear from *them*. More still are needed; surely, God will provide them too.

The nouthetic counseling group differs significantly from the psychoanalytic coterie with which Freud surrounded himself. For them to differ with the Master was heresy and it was necessary either to recant of anti-Freudian dogma or be excommunicated. No such relationship exists among nouthetic thinkers, all of whom are thinkers and theologians in their own right. They are yes *and no* men; and I learn continually from their nos. The chief difference lies in this: Freud — to preserve what he thought was truth — demanded utter allegience to his viewpoint. He could not do otherwise, since he himself was the final standard. We too have a Standard, but it is neither Jay Adams nor his writings. Our Standard is the Scriptures. The only heresy in nouthetic counseling, therefore, is abandonment of the teachings of that Book (and *not* that Book *as interpreted* by any one person — there is no infallible interpreter apart from the Holy Spirit). Therefore, nouthetic counselors, because they are encouraged to be true to the Scriptures, are *thereby encouraged to differ* with anyone, at any point where they believe with good cause that he deviates from the Scriptures or misinterprets them. But to be truly nouthetic a difference must be biblically based.

Thus a freedom (not bondage) of thoughts is fostered in nouthetic circles, a freedom as wide as the boundless spaces of the Word of the living God.

As I write I am excited to think of what may come forth from these men in the days ahead. I most sincerely hope that you will pray for, join forces with and support them in every way. I am convinced that they will produce the most substantive work of all.

CHAPTER TWO
PART ONE
COUNSELING AND THE SOVEREIGNTY OF GOD

Because it speaks to a number of critical issues that have been raised concerning nouthetic counseling, at this place I have included an address that I delivered on October 10, 1975 at Westminster Theological Seminary on the occasion of my inauguration as Professor of Practical Theology.[1] This address, in a more definitive manner speaks particularly of two matters of concern: theology and its importance in Christian counseling, and the relationship of pastoral counseling to psychiatry and psychology. Because it is current, I think also that the address may help to clarify the present stance of nouthetic counseling for some. Finally, since it places an emphasis upon the sovereignty of God — a factor that is critical to counseling — I believe that the address has importance in its own right, and therefore ought to be published.[2] So, for these three reasons, I have determined to release it — here.

INAUGURAL ADDRESS

A fourteen year old girl is abducted by a married man, the father of three children, who carries her off to an unknown destination. During the horror of the uncertain days that follow, what can sustain her parents? What is the supreme fact to which the Christian counselor can appeal that will bring hope and some measure of relief?

A family of seven, barely scraping along on the meager salary of a blue-collar worker in this inflationary era, suddenly is plunged into disaster by the closing down of the plant at which he works and his inability to obtain other work. They face the problem of survival

---

[1]Audio copies on cassette may be obtained from *Christian Study Services* , 1790 E. Willow Grove Ave., Laverock, Pa. 19118.

[2]The address appears also in *Lectures on Counseling,* a compilation of lectures and addresses that have been published separately.

amidst the uncertainties of a volatile world economy, poorly managed by greedy and godless men. How can the family survive this blow when a gallon of gasoline strikes a low of 54¢ and it is a bargain to buy three loaves of bread for a dollar? On what basis do they try to go on? Is there any use? Is there any meaning to it all? Any hope? To help them understand and cope with this dilemma what does their pastor tell them? To what bottom line truth should he point?

There is but one — the Sovereignty of God.

Knowing that God knows, that God cares, that God hears their prayers, and that God can and will act in His time and way to work even in this for good to His own...*that,* and nothing less than that conviction, can carry them through. And what that hope may be reduced to is a confident assurance that God is sovereign.

It has always been so.

When the problem of evil burned like an inextinguishable fire in his bones, and in the frustration of his situation, he cried for a personal hearing before God in order to vindicate himself and discover why he had become the object of such pain and sorrow, Job received one answer, and one alone. From out of the whirlwind came the final unequivocal word to be spoken concerning human suffering:

"I do in all the world according to my own good pleasure. *I* scattered the stars in the sky as *I* saw fit, and *I* created the beasts of the field and stream according to *My* desires. Job — where were you when all this took place? And who are you to question what I do with My own? I am sovereign."

In discussing the outcome of the remarkable course of history that through slavery and temptation and imprisonment at length raised him to the second highest political position in the world, Joseph assured his brothers:

"You did not send me here but God did" (Gen. 45:8).

And in a further affirmation, that was destined to become the Romans 8:28 of the Old Testament, he declared:

"You planned evil against me, but God planned it for good" (Gen. 50:20).

His firm conviction of this truth, doubtless growing stronger throughout the span of those hard days, was what made it all endurable.

When Moses protested that he could not undertake the task to which God was calling because of his slowness of speech, God did not acquiesce, argue or plead. He simply asserted His sovereignty in powerful words by means of a stinging statement: "Who made man's mouth?" (Ex. 4:11).

Under the most extreme sort of pressure to engage in idolatrous worship, Shadrach, Meshach and Abednego (according to the words of their unflinching testimony) rested solely upon the sovereignty of God:

"Our God," they said, "is able to deliver us" (Dan. 3:17).

And true to their word, in what may have been a preincarnate Christophany, that God in sovereign loving care walked through the fire with them.

In addition to these, others, who endured taunts and blows, fetters and prison, who were stoned to death, tortured, sawed in two, run through with the sword — *others,* I say, in faith rested upon the promises of a sovereign God whose Word they believed to be true, and whose promise they considered to be unfailing. Threat of death itself was not enough to shake their confidence in a *Sovereign* God.

Yes, it has always been that way; the sovereignty of God is the ultimate truth that meets human need. That is why the pastoral counselor, of all men, must believe this truth and search out its implications for each and every counseling situation.

And...that is why today, in the midst of the many modern crises that individuals and families undergo, the pastoral counselor who most assuredly affirms the sovereignty of God will bring the most significant help of all. Freudian fatalism, Rogerian humanism and Skinnerian evolutionary theory all fall woefully short of this help. Nothing less than this great truth can satisfy the longing heart or calm the troubled soul.

That is the way that it always has been, and that is the way that it always will be.

A counselor's theology, and his use of it in counseling, then, is neither a matter of indifference nor a question of insignificance. Rather, it is an issue of the most profound importance. Truth and godliness, the reality of God and the welfare of His people are inseparable. The godly man, who copes with life, is always the one who has appropriated God's truth for his life.

Take, for instance, the question on the lips of nearly every counselee — Why? Why did *this* have to happen? Why did it have to happen to *me*? Why did it have to happen *now*? Why? Why? Why?

Evolutionary explanations do not satisfy; they only aggravate. If man is no more than an animal, what hope is there? And of what significance is any attempt to change? The only value is the preservation of the herd.

Deistic determinism is no better. According to those who espouse such views, suffering merely follows as the inevitable consequence of the onward motion of impersonal law, in which the plight of the individual does not touch the heart of God since He has safely distanced Himself from His creation.

Existential embarrassment over the equivocation of a call to an authentic acknowledgment of the *absurd* can do no more than increase the pain.

Arminian answers that intimate that the problem may be a cause of frustration to God as well as to the counselee, only serve to point the discouraged, defeated disciple to a pathway that leads ultimately to atheism.

The only explanation that can fully set to rest this insistent human inquiry into the ultimate reason for the existence of misery and death is that the all powerful God who created and sustains this universe for His own good ends, sovereignly has decreed it.

By this reply, simultaneously are swept aside all notions of man in the clutches of a blind, impersonal force, every concept of a weak and unworthy deity who is to be pitied along with the rest of us because He can control His runaway world no longer, and any lingering suspicion that the destiny of a human being is nothing more than a move in a cosmic chess game in which he is as ruthlessly dispensed with as if he were a pawn — heedless of the welfare of any other piece than the King. He *is* sovereign; all *does* exist for the King. But this kingly God of creation plays the game according to His own rules. He is altogether sovereign and, therefore, the Originator of the game as well — rules and all. And as He faultlessly makes each move across the board, His strategy for winning the game involves the blessing of His loyal subjects as well as His own glory. And each subject, whose every hair is numbered, moves as He moves him in a responsible manner that He has sovereignly ordained.

So, you can see that a firm dependence upon the sovereignty of God is a dynamic concept in counseling — one that makes a difference, *the* difference — and, therefore, one that must undergird every effort at counseling. If, indeed, God is sovereign, ultimately all turns out well. All problems have solutions; every blighting effect of evil will be erased and all wrongs righted. The counselor who knows God as sovereign, has found fertile ground in which to plant his pastoral ministry. He will soon send down a tap root through which he will draw the living waters of life for many thirsty souls. Rooted and grounded in this foundational doctrine, his standpoint allows him freedom to view and to evaluate both the grand sweep of things and the plight of one poor sinner agonizing in the throes of personal grief. The sovereignty of God is the ground of hope and order in all that he does in counseling. It is the basis for all assurance that God's scriptural promises hold true. It is the cornerstone of Christian counseling.

But, before going any further, let me warn against two distinct, but dangerous tendencies of those who, while superficially holding the truth of the sovereignty of God, draw faulty implications from that great teaching. The biblical doctrine lends no support whatever either to those who, with near profanity, so glibly cry "Praise the Lord, anyway," in all sorts of inappropriate situations, nor does it provide comfort for mechanistic fatalists who wish to discount the idea of personal responsibility before God.

Taking the first matter seriously, there are at least two things to be said. On the one hand, counselors must affirm clearly that sin exists, and — along with it — that "misery" of which the catechisms so meaningfully speak. There can be no Christian Science-like denial of the stark tragedy of human existence since Adam. There can be no facile self-deception aimed at alleviating misery by attempting to conceal its true nature beneath a heap of pious expletives, symbolized in the phrase, "Praise the Lord, anyway." This vain effort, in the end, only lets one down hard. The counselor must give full recognition to sin and its terrifying effects if he wishes to be a faithful minster of the Lord Christ. After all, the Man of *Sorrows,* who was acquainted with *grief,* also believed in the sovereignty of God. Yet, He wept.

On the other hand, with equal vigor, every counselor worthy of the name of Christ, must impress upon his counselees the truth that the existence of a sovereign God is truly a cause for great joy and hope in the midst of tragedy and sorrow. For if God is sovereign, life is not absurd; it has design, a meaning and purpose.

Unlike existentialists, who vainly try to find meaning in man himself, the Christian pastoral counselor will show that this misdirected humanistic viewpoint is what constitutes the unbearable *angst* of which they so powerfully speak. Instead, the counselor directs the counselee's attention from creatures who, in Adam, have done little better than to get themselves involved in a kind of global Watergate affair before God. It is to the sovereign Creator and Sustainer of the universe, rather than to fallen creatures, that he bids the counselee to look for the final explanation that he seeks.

Apart from such a God, who knows the end from the beginning (because He ordained it), human beings cannot explain their existence because they have no eschatology; death ends all. But, in Him, there is a *denouement.* There will be an ultimate disclosure of the unrevealed particulars of His divine purpose. Those things that now so often seem to be but meaningless functions in the course of human activity will all come alive with significance. Each piece of the puzzle will be put in place at last — the dark purples of despair, the fiery reds of anger and affliction, the sickly yellows — and we shall be permitted to view the whole as it now exists in the plan of God alone. The comforting conviction that there is a beautiful, meaningful picture on the cover of life's puzzle box to which each piece of distress and pain bears a faithful resemblance, belongs solely to those who affirm the sovereignty of God. Without such a conviction, there is no hope.

Likewise, one can escape the fear of a disorderly world, relentlessly rolling on like an avalanche that is out of control, only by an adherence to the doctrine of the sovereignty of God. Because of the certainty of order and control that the doctrine requires, even crazy and bizarre behavior in human beings is not inexplicable to the Christian counselor. Behind its baffling facade lies an etiology that can be traced immediately to personal rebellion against God and His laws, or (as a physiological consequence of Adam's sin) may extend all of the way back to Eden. Either way he knows that deviant human thought and action is not the result of mere chance. It is explicable in terms of a violated covenant and the judgment of a personal God.

Thus hope wells up in the heart of every man to whom God reveals Himself savingly, for there is One who came to pay the penalty for the broken law and to keep covenant with the Father. Because of His perfect fulfillment of all that God demands, men may be saved here and hereafter from the penalty and from the grip of sin. Ultimately, the evil consequences of sin will be removed altogether from the lives and from the environment of the redeemed. Indeed, so great will be the effects of salvation that those who were created lower than the angels, will in Christ be raised far above by His grace. They will share with Him in His glory. So, you see, there is meaning in it all, after all. Where sin abounded, grace more fully abounds. Even the absurd and the bizarre take on meaning as the foil against which the glory of God's grace may best be displayed.

And, lastly, there is hope also in the face of God's sovereignty because His is a personal rule over His subjects. The atonement, by which the redeemed were reconciled to God, was no impersonal or abstract transaction, as if Christ died for "mankind." He is a *personal* Savior, who loved particular individuals and shed His blood for them.

Cicero, in *De Natura Deorum* (2:66) wrote: "Magna di curant, parva neglegunt." ("The gods are concerned with important things; trifles they ignore.") No such God is the sovereign God of our salvation. A sick child was of no consequence to Venus or Aphrodite. Larger questions — like some of the ongoing rivalries and disputes with the gods and other goddesses of the Greek and

Roman pantheons — occupied their time and attention. Such gods brought no comfort or hope to men, because they were not sovereign. Much of creation slipped by beyond their purview. But there is hope in the presence of the true Sovereign because He is in control of everything. Not a sparrow falls without Him. He is the God of trifles. Jesus taught us by His works and words what this sovereign God is like. The way that He put it was:

"He who has seen me has seen the Father."

And, it is in that very Gospel of John in which these words are recorded that we are so pointedly shown Jesus' deep concern for individuals — Nicodemus, the woman at the well, the blind man, Lazarus, Mary and Martha.... It is in the same Gospel that we hear Him speak of His shepherdly concern; a concern that extends to the hundredth sheep and that calls each by name. The sovereign Shepherd of Israel is great enough to care about trifles — like us! He labors under none of the limitations of the classical gods. Nor does He stand at a deistic distance in disinterest. This sovereign God is the Father of a redeemed family over which He exercises total care and concern. There is plenty of hope for every Christian counselor in that.

Moving now along a continuum full of factors that might command our attention, I suggest that we pause for a moment to urge every pastoral counselor to remember the sobering fact that the existence of a God who is sovereign neither removes nor lessens, but (rather) *establishes* human responsibility to that God. If He who is sovereign over all men and over all their actions has determined that they shall be responsible to Him, then that settles it. That is how it is when a sovereign Creator speaks. It does not matter whether it is difficult to reconcile responsibility with sovereignty or not, because that is precisely what God decreed: Men shall be responsible to Him! And if He sovereignly determined to create man as a being fashioned in His image and governed by His moral law...so be it! That is the prerogative of a sovereign God.

Shall the pot say to the potter, "Why have you made me thus?" When you stop to think about it, to whom could one be more responsible than to the One who created him and sustains his every breath. To put it another way — because God is sovereign, He is the *only* one who is not responsible to another. Did not the Lamb of God Himself, who according to the sovereign plan of God was "slain from the foundation of the world," nevertheless declare:

"It is proper for us to fulfill all righteousness"?

That statement presupposes responsibility.

It should be eminently clear, then, that God's sovereignty neither encourages the utterance of pietistic platitudes like "praise the Lord, anyway" as the solution to the problem of human suffering, nor does it leave us unaccountable. Indeed, it is this very truth that *demands* of us nothing less than a realistic eyes-wide-open response to the existential situations of life, for God will hold us answerable both as counselors and counselees.

All counseling that measures up to the biblical standard, must fully acknowledge both the tragedy of sin and the fact of human responsibility. It must reckon with God's ultimate purpose to glorify Himself in His Son and in a people redeemed by His grace. While all things will turn out well, they do so, not apart from, but precisely because of the responsible action of the Son of God who came and actually died for those who from all eternity had been ordained to eternal life.

It should be obvious that I have not attempted to open up the many practical implications of the doctrine of God's sovereignty in any concrete way. The doctrine is so foundational that the number of such implications is large. I wish rather to invite others of you to join with me in extracting the ore from this virtually untouched mine.

The sovereignty of God has been taught and preached, it is true — largely in an abstract way — but little has been done to explore the applications of this doctrine for life, and (therefore) for counseling. Moreover, Christian counseling has failed to measure up to its name principally because its early theorists were unskilled in exegesis and theology. Largely, they came to counseling through a background of psychology. Yet as important as psychology (rightly conceived and practiced) may be, it can never be foundational to counseling, but only ancillary.

Counseling — as we shall see — has to do with the counselee's relationship to persons. God, and all the others who people his horizon, are its concern. Only incidentally does the counselor concern himself with other matters. Clearly love for God and one's neighbor is a prime interest of the minister of the Word.

That is why here at Westminster Theological Seminary over the past ten years the attempt has been made to teach pastoral counseling from the starting point of God's sovereignty. In everything that has been done and every word that has been written, it has been our goal to take that doctrine seriously, following its implications obediently, no matter where they might lead. Often the road has proven both difficult and unpopular; yet travel along it always has been satisfying. Temptations to veer to the right or to the left have been numerous. It has not always been easy to resist them. God alone knows how well we have succeeded in doing so.

"But," you inquire, "can you tell me more about the ways in which the doctrine of God's sovereignty has affected the theory and practice of the teaching of counseling at Westminster?" The basic answer to your question is this: Both theory and practice have been affected in *every* way.

But to become more concrete, let me mention what I consider to be the most significant influence the doctrine has exerted, an influence that has had marked effect upon both theory and practice. Early in the development of a counseling stance from which to teach, the question of encyclopedia arose. To what task does the pastoral counselor address himself? In counseling, does he handle a very narrow band of "spiritual" or "ecclesiastical" problems, or is his field of legitimate activity substantially larger? Is his counseling activity bordered (and thereby limited) by others from clearly distinct disciplines, namely psychologists and psychiatrists (whose titles, curiously enough, might be translated not too freely — as "soul specialists" and "soul healers")?

Over the years the question always has been kept in view. Gradually, the Scriptures have driven us to an answer — an answer that one hardly would have chosen by himself. The conviction has grown that it is God's answer. And when God speaks by His inerrant word, what He says is *Sovereign*.

Because of the teaching of the Scriptures, one is forced to conclude that much of clinical and counseling psychology, as well as most of psychiatry, has been carried on without license from God and in autonomous rebellion against Him. This was inevitable because the Word of the sovereign God of creation has been ignored.

In that Word are "all things pertaining to life and godliness." By it the man of God "may be fully equipped for every good work." And it is that Word — and only that Word — that can tell a poor sinner how to love God with all of the heart, and mind, and soul, and how to love a neighbor with the same depth of concern that he exhibits toward himself. On these two commandments hang all the law and prophets. They are the very summation of God's message to the world and to His redeemed people. And, as a consequence, it is the calling of the shepherds of God's flock (*par excellence*) to guide the sheep into the pathways of loving righteousness for His Name's sake. Putting it that way — that God's Name is at stake — shows the importance of this task.

"All of that sounds quite biblical and...it all sounds very innocuous," you may say. "But," you continue, "I don't see where that puts psychologists and psychiatrists in conflict with God. You'd better explain that one more fully." O.K. Let me screw the two things together for you so that you can see the interconnection that leads to the conflict.

In assigning the pastor the task of helping sheep to learn how to love God and neighbor, God has spoken sovereignly. If this is the pastor's task, clearly delineated in the Bible, then he must pursue it. This puts him in the counseling business. But, immediately, upon surveillance of the field, he discovers all sorts of other persons already out there trying to do similar things, and saying that to them — not to him — belongs the task of counseling. There are competitors in the vicinity. Indeed, even a cursory investigation indicates that they are not merely in the vicinity but in the sheepfold itself. And, as a result, the true shepherd soon discovers that they are leading the sheep astray.

"But," you ask, "is there no basic difference between the work done by psychologists and psychiatrists, and that done by a pastor?" There is no way to distinguish between the work of the pastor as it is sovereignly ordered in the Scriptures, and that which is attempted by others who lay claim to the field. Persons who come to counselors for help are persons who are having difficulty with persons. They don't come complaining, "You see, I've got this problem with my carburetor." That is why love for God (*the* Person) and for one's neighbor are such vital factors in counseling. Nothing could be more central to a pastor's concern. Yet, it is with this concern about persons that psychologists and psychiatrists also busy themselves. They want to change persons and the relationships between persons.

I contend, therefore, that it is not the pastor who is responsible for the overlap; it is the psychologist on the one side, who has moved his fence over onto the pastor's territory, and the psychiatrist on the other, who also has encroached upon his property. Unfortunately, until recently, pastors have been all too willing to allow others to cut their grass. At long last, largely under the impetus of the Westminster emphasis, there has been a noticeable change in attitude by conservative pastors everywhere.

"Now, wait a minute. Are you saying that psychology and psychiatry are illegitimate disciplines? Do you think that they have no place at all?"

No, you misunderstand me. It is exactly not that. Remember, I said clearly that they live next door to the pastor. My problem with them is that they refuse to stay on their own property. I have been trying to get the pastor to mow his lawn to the very borders of his plot.

Psychology should be a legitimate and very useful neighbor to the pastor. Psychologists may make many helpful studies of man (e.g., on the effects of sleep loss). But psychologists — with neither warrant nor standard from God by which to do so — should get out of the business of trying to change persons. Psychology may be descriptive, but transgresses its boundaries whenever it becomes prescriptive. It can tell us many things about what man does, but not about what he should do.

Similarly, the neighbor who lives on the other side of the pastor's lot could be a most welcome one with whom the pastor could live in real harmony were he satisfied to play croquet in his own yard. Psychiatrists, for the most part, are a tragic lot. I say this not only because among the professions psychiatrists have the highest suicide rate, but more fundamentally because they are persons highly trained in skills that they hardly use, and instead spend most of their time doing what they were never adequately trained to do. In the United States psychiatrists are physicians, who (for the most part) use their medical training to do little else than prescribe pills. Freud, himself, acknowledged that a background in medicine is not required for the practice of psychiatry. That is why in other parts of the world psychiatrists are not necessarily medical persons. And that is why clinical and counseling psychologists do the same things as psychiatrists without specialized training as physicians.

The pastor recognizes the effects of Adam's sin upon the body; he, therefore, has no problem working side-by-side with a physician who treats the counselee's body as he counsels him about its proper use. From the days of Paul and Luke, pastors have found kinship with medical personnel. Why, then, does the psychiatrist present a problem? Certainly it is not because of his medical background. The problem is that he will not stay in his own backyard. He keeps setting up his lawn chairs and moving his picnic table onto the pastor's property.

If he were to use his medical training to find medical solutions to the truly organic difficulties that affect attitudes and behavior, the pastor would be excited about his work. But the difficulty arises as the psychiatrist — under the guise of medicine — attempts to change values and beliefs. That is not medicine. The pastor is disturbed at having residents from the adjoining lots digging up his backyard to plant corn and tomatoes. He does not object — but rather encourages — all such activity in the yards next door.

So, in effect, the issue boils down to this: the Bible is the text book for living before God and neighbor, and the pastor has been ordained to teach and guide God's flock by it. When others try to take over the work, and substitute other text books, conflict is inevitable. The most recent change has occurred because the pastor has taken a fresh look at his title deed, and resurveyed the land. In the process he has discovered an incredible amount of usurpation by others. He dare not abandon the tract to which God in the Scriptures has given him a clear title. The idea is not to destroy psychology or psychiatry, pastors simply want psychologists and psychiatrists to cultivate their own property.

In all of this, the sovereignty of God has played the conspicuous role. So often, however, when thinking of His sovereignty, we restrict our concern to the matter of the relation of regeneration to faith. But it is not only in regeneration that God is sovereign; He is sovereign in sanctification as well. If, in order to accomplish His purpose in the believer, He has given His Word to be ministered by His church in the power of His Spirit, that is how these purposes must be accomplished; there can be no other way. And pastors, as key persons in all of this, must see to it that this is the way that things are done — whether it pleases others or not. The ministry of the Word to believers in counseling can be dispensed with no more readily than the ministry of the Word in preaching.

In conclusion, therefore, I wish to emphasize the fact that what has been going on in the practical theology department at Westminster in the area of counseling, has been issued from a tight theological commitment. The position that has been developed and articulated is the direct result of Reformed thinking. Those who hold to other theological commitments, it might be noted, have viewed the problems in the field quite differently. Because of their failure to acknowledge the sovereignty of God at other points, they cannot hold the line against the defection of autonomous thought and action in counseling either. So, if there is anything that has been done here over the last decade that is worthy of mention, it is but the natural outcome of the faithful efforts of those who labored before. For it was they who, against unthinkable odds, held tenaciously to, and in clarity and with power delineated, the scriptural truth of the sovereignty of God in all things. The principles that they taught us we now are making every effort to apply to the task of Christian counseling.

We call upon you whoever you are, and in whatever way you can — to join with us in this work. It has just begun. During the next ten years far more can be accomplished if you do. The needs are great; the opportunities are numerous; the human resources are few. We would stagger at the enormity of the undertaking but for one fact. It is a fact that brings hope and confidence; a fact that is the source of all humility and gratitude, —

It is the fact that God is Sovereign.

PART TWO

DO YOU REALLY BELIEVE THAT?

As I said earlier, there have been a number of misrepresentations of the nouthetic viewpoint, not only by its enemies, but sometimes even by its friends. For this reason I am anxious to answer some of the questions that have been raised, hoping that by means of these replies I shall be able to clarify my position and once more — in a pointed way — set forth some of the truths of the Bible that are pertinent to Christian counseling.

The questions that follow are selective. Questions that you may wish to raise may not be considered.[1] Moreover, I have determined to limit my responses to rather short answers. Longer ones would defeat the purpose of this book, which is to make a brief, but pointed, informative thrust forward at this transitional time. It is my hope that brevity will help rather than further confuse or complicate the situation. I have found that even when I have taken great pains to qualify my statements, reviewers often miss these qualifications altogether. It is perhaps better, then, to come right to the point, and say what I have to say as tersely and as flatfootedly as possible. That is the style that I have chosen in the present section.

---

[1] I have been working on the preparation of a much larger text dealing with a great number of questions in a more systematic fashion. In that book, I hope (D.V.) to consider almost every question that I have ever been asked about nouthetic counseling. It will be sometime before I can publish it, however.

1. Question: Do you think that feelings are unimportant?

Answer: Of course not! They play vital roles in the human make-up. Nothing about man is unimportant. Every aspect of man serves a purpose that God ordained; that is why it is important. But, the importance of each aspect differs according to function and context. Just as the eye is important for seeing and the ear for hearing, other aspects of the human personality have their special importance too. But precisely because of its very special functions the ear is unimportant for seeing and the eye for hearing. So, too, while one may recognize the vital place of the feelings, he also may argue for their relative lack of importance for particular functions in a certain context. Indeed, as you can see, it may be harmful so to stress the importance of one aspect of man out of its proper context. (Don't try to determine whether the traffic light is green or red by using your ear; you'd better use your eye!)

Most of the misrepresentations of nouthetic confrontation having to do with the feelings, suggest (as the question implies) that nouthetic counselors think that feelings are not important. This is a gross error. I, therefore, should like to repudiate it with all the vigor that words can command: feelings *are* important, indeed, without feelings man would be something less than a man. For instance, without feelings, conscience would not function, there would be no warning of danger; life would lose its zest and joy, there would be no tenderness — feelings *are* important.

But with equal vigor let me emphasize the unimportance of feelings. Feelings cannot be allowed to function in place of other capacities any more than the eye may be used to hear or the ear to see. Nouthetic confrontation has not underplayed feelings; it has attempted to put them in their proper place. What I have fought in a feeling-oriented age is the emphasis upon *wrong* uses of the feelings.

What are the functions of feeling, and what are some of the erroneous ways in which these have been missed and in which feelings have been substituted for other human capacities?

Let me suggest two things (these are selective, not exhaustive, replies):

1. Feelings wrongly have been accepted as the guide for life. Expressions like "Follow your feelings," "If it feels right, do it," and

"I can't if I don't *feel* like it" are rife. The Christian's guide, however, is *not* his feelings; it is the Bible. Any whisper to the contrary in counseling, any hint that feelings constitute an additional or even another (though lesser) guide for Christian living must be resisted. I have discussed the reasons for this in detail in *The Christian Counselor's Manual* and will not attempt to duplicate them here. Shun like the plague all feeling oriented counseling approaches that make feelings the guide for counselor or counselee.

2. Feelings are not the principal point of focus for the Christian counselor. While the counselee often is strongly motivated by his feelings to seek help — and this is good (negative feelings have been built into man's personality by God as warning and motivating factors and are of great importance in this respect)[2] — nevertheless, the biblical solution to his problem rarely can be reached by attempting to alter his feelings. The change of feelings will take place when the change of attitude or behavior has been effected. This takes place because the counselee judges that the change of attitude or behavior is good. This judgment triggers better feelings. Pills may obstruct the feeling mechanisms, but they cannot change the facts or the evaluation of them. The counselor, therefore, realizes that he must seek to bring about more basic change in the Christian. This change occurs at the level of *obedience* to the Word of God through the power of the Spirit who works in and through His inspired revelation to bring about such change. He does not command the believer to change his feelings but to change his attitudes and behavior. Human beings have not been constructed in such a way that it is possible to obey a command to change feelings unaided.[3] That is why the counselor focuses on *obedience to the Word of God* rather than feelings.[4] It does not mean that feelings are unimportant.

---

[2] This is a chief reason why the modern symptomatic treatment of human difficulties by the use of pills, E.C.T. and other means of deactivating feelings is so dangerous.

[3] By means of bio-feedback feelings can be controlled on demand. I wish to discuss this important consideration at another place.

[4] Some (e.g., Larry Crabb) think I underplay the cognitive aspects of counseling. With all of my emphasis on data gathering, explanation of the Scriptures, etc. I fail to see how they can get this idea. Behavior cannot be encouraged apart from understanding. One must know what and how before he can act. All my books focus on this. One wonders, at times, if others truly read what I have written.

2. Question: Why don't you say more about empathy?

Answer: Because I have said enough already. "Enough?" you may reply. "Why I hardly read anything about this in your books." Correct. If you are asking for long dissertations on the subject, or for pages of hortatory material encouraging empathy, you will not find that in my writings. Yet that is not the only, nor in my opinion, the proper way of writing about empathy. Note also that the Bible is overtly slim on the subject. I believe that this scriptural silence may be accounted for in one way only; the Bible does not emphasize empathy for exactly the same reason that I do not — *there is no need to do so.* If one person counsels another nouthetically (note the three elements in such counseling)[5] then *by virtue of using such an approach he will be empathetic.*

Exhortations and explanations about empathy do not bring it about. Empathy occurs when one deeply involves himself in the life, problems or work of another. He does not wait to *become empathetic* first — then involve himself; rather the opposite is true. The sort of involvement integral to nouthetic counseling at once *necessarily* requires and fosters empathy. Nouthetic counseling, because of the depth of involvement, actually might be said to be the *only* counseling that is truly empathetic. Only nouthetic counselors can properly weep with those who weep and rejoice with those who rejoice.

All those who *talk* about empathy do not necessarily have it. Empathy cannot be tacked on to one's counseling, as some writings seem to indicate; instead it must be an integral part of the counseling process. Indeed, one wonders whether many of those who talk and write so fully about it, and those who seek so earnestly to attain it, do not do so precisely because the system by which they counsel, does not actually require or (perhaps) even allow for it. Those who already have something do not need to continually talk about *seeking* for it.

Empathy is the outgrowth of rejoicing with those who do and weeping with those who do. White coated, professionalized systems that prohibit this are restrictive of empathetic dealings. Moreover,

---

[5]Cf. especially *Competent to Counsel,* pp. 49ff. The third element particularly embraces the concept.

empathy cannot merely be *felt*: it must be *shown* toward another by one's actions. Sympathy (suffering or feeling *with*) can be *felt*; empathy (suffering or feeling in) necessitates an entering into the situation as a participant who, himself, has become *involved*. That is of the essence in nouthetic counseling. I'll close with a parable.

Picture a man under his automobile pulling on a wrench. A would-be empathetic type approaches. He speaks:

"What's the problem?"

"Agh...I can't get this nut loose."

"That's a shame. I suppose that's frustrating isn't it?"

"Yeah...."

"I'm trying to enter into your problem. I can feel what you feel, struggle with what you're struggling with...."

"Look, will you please get out of here; I'm having enough trouble with this nut."

Now picture a nouthetic counselor coming by:

"What's the problem?"

"Agh...I can't get this nut loose."

"Wait a minute, let me get my coat off and get under there and help you."

Which of these men do you think was empathetic — the one who talked about empathy or the one who showed empathy?

3. Question: Don't you believe in any kind of mental illness?

Answer: It depends on what you mean by those words. If you mean that brain damage, brain abscess, tumors on the brain, meningitis of the brain, hardening of the arteries or insufficient oxygen to the brain can so alter the physical state of the brain that one's behavior is significantly affected by it, of course I believe in mental illness. Those disorders that I have listed, and a number of others like them, are true physical illnesses. It is perfectly clear that such illnesses can and do affect behavior. In such instances, medical help should be sought and administered prayerfully.

But there is another, much more common use of the words *mental illness.* What confuses many persons is that both ideas usually are carelessly lumped together under that term rather than distinguished from one another. This second use actually is quite deceptive, for (in the final analysis) it is a contradiction of terms. According to this second usage, mental illness is conceived as a condition in which the victim (almost always in one way or another the victim motif is used)[6] has contracted an *inorganic* illness (whatever that may be) as the result of *inorganic* causes that must be treated by *inorganic* means.

But what is an illness if it is inorganic? Physicians are body-oriented persons. The fact is that the illness/medical terminology (sickness, patient, treatment, therapy, etc.) actually is used figuratively or euphemistically. An inorganic illness (or disease) is a contradiction in terms. In no other than a figurative sense could one be said to have a disease or illness unless his *body* were ill. Disease is an organic concept. In the second usage, a figure of speech has been taken literally.

When psychiatrists talk about relationships, values, socialization, attitudes, behavior, etc., they let the cat out of the bag; they are not dealing with illnesses at all! In actuality, they are not doing medical work. The medical terminology may lend a certain kind of ethos and authority to what they do, but if and when it does, in the long run, that happens only by deceiving the counselee. That deception may be conscious or unconscious, well-meaning or otherwise. The

---

[6]This motif removes responsibility.

reason is not my concern here; I am concerned about the effect. Either way, it is achieved only by the erroneous assumptions made by the counselee when he is told that his problem comes from "mental illness" and must be treated by "competent medical (or 'professional') help."

Of greatest importance is the fact that the illness concept, and in particular, the victim theme[7] ("your parents did this to you"), takes away personal responsibility. Who blames anyone for contracting an illness (chicken pox, let us say)?

I have written quite fully on this point elsewhere so I shall not extend this answer.[8] Much more might be said (such as noting the unkindness of the victim/illness model in contrast to the sin model). But see *Competent to Counsel, The Big Umbrella* and *The Christian Counselor's Manual* for further information on this and various other aspects of this question.

---

[7]Along with its blame-shifting emphasis.

[8]I hope too, in a future volume, to examine the importance of language in counseling.

4. Question: Do you believe that all of our problems are due to sin?

Answer: Yes and no. That is not an equivocal answer; the question is imprecise and, therefore, requires such an answer.

Yes, all problems are the consequence of sin, if by that one means that *ultimately* they have the sin of Adam (or Satan) as their ultimate cause. All personal differences with God or neighbor ultimately stem from that cause. All bodily afflictions, and death itself go back to that source.

But I must say *no* in response to the question if by it one means that all sickness, all evils that he confronts, and all difficulties and distresses that he experiences in life are directly traceable to some *immediate* sinful cause in the life of the one who undergoes them. That is not a biblical concept. The case of the blind man in John 9 gives the lie to any such notion, and the entire book of Job is a sturdy witness to the contrary.

At the same time, it is quite possible that in many cases such a direct relationship does exist. James 5:14-16[9] and I Corinthians 11:29,30 give sufficient evidence of the fact that much sickness and trouble does come as the direct result of one's specific sin (and, in both of these instances this is seen to be true of the believer).

---

[9]But notice particularly the "if" in vs. 15. The possibility is thus acknowledged without insisting that all sickness is so caused.

5. Question: Don't you think that we can learn something from psychologists?

Answer: Yes, we can learn a lot; I certainly have. That answer surprised you, didn't it? If it did, you have been led to believe, no doubt, that nouthetic counselors are obscurantists who see no good in psychology. Or perhaps you have been told that they are sadly self-deceived persons who, while decrying all psychology, take many of their ideas from psychologists without knowing it. Both charges are preposterous.

While I can understand how the idea that I am opposed to psychology and psychologists could have gotten abroad because of my strong statements about the failures of psychologists *as counselors,* a *careful* reading of my materials will make it clear that I do not object to psychology or to psychologists as such. My objections are directed solely to so-called clinical and counseling psychology in which most of what is done I consider not to be the work or province of psychology at all. That I deplore psychology's venture into the realms of value, behavior and attitudinal change because it is an intrusion upon the work of the minister, in no way lessens my interest, support and encouragement of the legitimate work of psychology.

I have profited greatly, for instance, from the results of the work done at the Harvard sleep labs (and elsewhere). This sleep study I consider to be a valid and worthwhile enterprise for psychology. Indeed, I wish all psychologists would go back to such work.

But when psychologists attempt to change men, although they have no warrant from God to do so, no standard by which to determine what are proper or deviant attitudes or behavior, no concept of what man *should* look like, and no power by which to achieve the inner changes of heart and thought that are so necessary, I cannot help but be concerned.

I would not oppose psychiatrists either if they were doing the important medical work that it is necessary to do to help people whose behavior is adversely affected by organic causes.

6. Question: What do you mean by confrontation?

Answer: I'm glad that you asked that question because from the feedback thus far I find that for some persons (perhaps a large number) this word has rather negative connotations. Let me say right away that for me it does not.

The word confrontation, as I have used it in such phrases as *nouthetic confrontation* or *confront nouthetically* has a strongly positive flavor. I might almost as readily have said "to consult with nouthetically," or I might have spoken of "nouthetic consultation."[10] The basic thrust of the word confrontation has always been to indicate personal face to face involvement that refuses to sidestep the often unpleasant but necessary task of helping a person who is in difficulty.

Presumably, for some, there clusters about this word ideas of nastiness or belligerency. Nothing could be farther from my mind as I use it. However, there is an authoritative element in the term confrontation that rightly conveys the idea that biblical counseling has something of importance to say. Because he counsels on the basis of the Scriptures, the counselor's stance is not that of a mere consultant, but rather that of a servant of God acting as a prophet, speaking forth the Word of God that applies to the need at hand. That is confrontation. Persons, such as Rogerians, who have difficulty with the very idea of authority in counseling, naturally will object to the use of the word confrontation. But we cannot abandon the biblical concept because of their objections. The word nouthetic attached to the word confrontation is also of importance. This clearly qualifies the kind of confrontation in view.

---

[10]The word *consultation,* however, is too neutral. The positive aggressiveness and the willingness to put one's self on the line in reaching out to help another in a face to face encounter that is inherent in *nouthesia* is better expressed by the word confrontation. For me it is a good and *more* positive term than consultation. Moreover, consultation says nothing about who directs the conversation.

7. Question: Why are you so critical of the views of others?

Answer: We are not always critical, nor do we criticize everyone. But nouthetic counselors have been critical; that is correct.

Why? Well, let me say at the outset, not because we enjoy it. It is not pleasant to have to differ with others. That has nothing to do with it. If this were the motivating factor behind our work, there would be more negative than positive material in what I have published. But that is not the case. I have made no criticisms without offering positive, biblical alternatives. I have tried never to smash a window unless I had a better one with which to replace it. This is a crucial point, sometimes lost by those who deplore all negative criticism. Furthermore, the amount of positive teaching in my books far outweighs the amount of negative criticism. I am convinced that this all-important factor has blunted the point of many counterattacks (very few of which have had any positive content). Nouthetic counseling never has been and never will be (so long as it stays true to its principles)[11] critical for criticism's sake.

Then why do you engage in so much criticism? Fundamentally, for three reasons:

1. To warn the Christian Church about the grave dangers of the inroads of godless counseling systems into the life of the church.

2. To show that non-biblical systems of counseling cannot cut the mustard because they have ignored the Bible — God's textbook for counseling — and therefore must be abandoned. To be true to God and His Word, one *must* call attention to this crucial fact.

3. To urge (unfortunately *against* prevailing views) ministers of the gospel in particular, and Christians in general, to get back into the work of counseling to which they were called by God.

If and when the nouthetic counseling movement should cease to provide scriptural help and turns merely to critical efforts, then it too will receive my criticism, together (of course) with biblical alternatives!

Ask any pastor who is acquainted with the various systems to tell

---

[11]Note particularly the nouthetic principle that we must not focus upon problems only, but soon move to God's solutions.

you who he thinks has worked hardest to provide him with the most concrete how-to-help in counseling. I think that an unbiased reply will single out the nouthetic approach above all of the others. Who (in the long run) is making the most *positive* impact — nouthetic counselors or those who, while criticizing nouthetic counselors as critical, make little or no concrete effort to help others to become better counselors?

8. Question: Are you sure that Freud, Rogers, Skinner, et al are competing with the pastor and trying to carry on activities that overlap and usurp his?

Answer: Yes, and because I have shown why this conviction is sound both in this book and elsewhere, I shall append only one *additional* reason for that assertion at this point. Although it is a single reason, it is an extremely important one, and so I make no apology for answering so vital a question with this lone reply. Perhaps its fundamental nature will stand out all the more as the result.

Counselors of every description, by virtue of the work that they seek to do, are compelled to think, speak, decide and act theologically. Even though nearly all of them would steer as wide a course around theological issues as they could, and although they would protest that what they are doing is not theology, it is impossible for them to do so. The very stuff of which counseling is made (how to live a human life in this fallen sinful world that God made for His glory) *requires* theological responses.

It is true that few recognize the theological necessities or implications of their discussions, commitments and endeavors, and of course, they rarely use theological language.[12] But that is beside the point. If one is doing theology he is doing it (1) whether he is aware of it or not, (2) whether he speaks in theological terminology or not and (3) whether it is good theology or bad. When theological activities are done unconsciously that must mean that they will be done poorly. Yet, those issues are irrelevant. The main point is that those who are involved in theological activities simply are involved in theological activities.

"But what do you mean?" you may ask. "How is Carl Rogers doing theology? I thought he was opposed to any such thing." You are quite correct about his opposition to theology. But opposition to theology is itself an intensely theological stance. It is a stance that says that God is not needed in solving man's problems. That viewpoint is theological. It is bad theology, I'll grant you, but it is

---

[12]O. Hobart Mowrer is an exception. Yet even he tried to use theological language as a skin to fit his humanistic beliefs.

theology. Every such statement that is made about man, his problems and the solutions to them is theological. If one believes that at the core of his person man is essentially good, as Rogers claims, his belief is a theological one that has far-reaching implications, touching all of the theological doctrines of the fall of man, sin, revelation, the atonement, etc. There is nothing atheological at all about such a commitment.

Moreover, if (as Rogers avers) the solution to man's problems lies in the realization of his own inner potential, that is a theological commitment which, if it were true, would vitiate the whole plan of salvation and make the cross of Christ a cruel mockery or (at best) a futile waste and a deceitful lie.

If, with Rogers, the goal of counseling is to make man autonomous (a word with positive connotations for him) rather than dependent on God, His Word and his brothers and sisters in Christ, that too has dramatic theological impact.

So, all that Rogers says and does about man's condition and how to alter it by counseling is theological whether he understands this or not. You can't talk about man, his condition and the solutions to his problems without becoming *deeply* involved in theology. In one sense, ignoring God in all of this is the most theological thing one can do!

The same sort of extended analysis could be made of every counseling system. Of course, that can't be done here where brevity is our concern. But note briefly a few things about a couple of them. When Freud says that man is not responsible for what he does, when he claims that man is really motivated by the irrational 9/10 of the iceberg below the surface, when he sides with the sinful impulses of human nature (as he calls it, the *id*) against conscience (for him, the *superego*), and then tries to sear the conscience with the hot irons of psychotherapy, such beliefs and activities are thoroughly theological.

Skinner's concerns to eliminate all mentalistic and ghostly concepts and language like value, dignity, God, salvation, spirit, etc., his reductionistic attempt to prove that all that goes on in man is behavior, and his view that man is only an animal are all theological. Skinner's poor theology denies the uniqueness of man's creation in God's image. That certainly is a theological stance from any theologian's point of view!

If a Christian, by reading these lines, cannot see the essentially theological nature of the counselor's task, I don't know how to make it clearer to him. The moment a counselor speaks of beliefs, values, behavior, change, problems, solutions, human relationships and other such matters he is knee deep in theology. Whether he knows this or not is irrelevant. One doesn't need to know that he is breathing air to do so! All value judgments boil down to theological judgments. All attempts to change man necessarily require some view of what man is, what he is now, what he ought to become and how. That is theology!

Such matters can't be discussed by a Christian apart from biblical theology (i.e., apart from what God says about these issues in the Bible[13]). While unbelieving counselors or counseling theorists cannot be expected to see this (cf. Rom. 1:18ff; II Cor. 4:4), there is no excuse for Bible-believing Christians, pastors and seminary professors to miss the point.

---

[13] At bottom, that is what Christian theology is.

9. Question: Why don't you write more fully about the counselor as a godly man?

Answer: It is necessary, perhaps, to say a word about the relationship of the counselor to God. In my books, I assume much that I do not spell out because I think that enough has been written about such matters already and my concern always has been to break new ground, to fill in holes and (in general) to do what yet needs to be done. Life is too short to take the time to duplicate what has been done well already.

I must admit, however, that this concern of mine has resulted in a certain sort of imbalance in my writings that allows those who wish to make a point of it to do so. But, again, I have been writing not to convince the opposition but to help those who want guidance. I don't need to make points in this sort of writing. And, I have found that when my reader has no axe to grind, and is operating on the same biblical wave lengths that I am, he understands and even appreciates the fact that I try not to waste his time reading truisms and material he can pick up anywhere. At least hundreds of pastors have told me this. Since the first chapters of nearly every pastoral counseling book, every preaching text and every pastoral work volume contain exhortations about what sort of man a minister should be, I have not tried to duplicate this.

As a result, my writings don't abound in exhortations to counselors to become godly men themselves (although here and there, by the way that I touch on the subject obliquely, and sometimes more directly, it has not been very difficult for those who want to read fairly to discover my underlying views about these matters). That they should continuously strive to build into their own lives those things that they must call upon their counselees to do goes without saying. So I haven't spent a lot of space saying it. Yet all that I have written about the pastor as an example or model (and this has been a good bit) indicates the importance of the counselor's own life.

But has this resulted in a serious omission profoundly needing remedy? Do our trainees go away as hypocrites, bent on telling everyone else what to do, yet heedless of their own sins?

No! Indeed, one of the most common responses that we get from those who have completed our counselor's training program at CCEF[14] is something like this: "Not only did I profit from what I learned about counseling, but this course has changed my life," or "My whole relationship to God and my wife has changed as a result of this course," or "Perhaps the most important effect of this course has been the way in which it has changed my own life." And note, these comments are entirely unsolicited. (We don't have times of reflection and evaluation at the end where each person gives a testimony about what has happened during his ten weeks' study at the center; rather we study and work till the very last moment.) And these unsolicited comments continually come. Why?

The answer to the question with which the previous paragraph ends is (in part, at least) that Christian counseling deals with problems of living life God's way. We do not give counsel about how to tune the engine on a brand new Audi; we talk about how to love God and one's neighbor. This cuts a wide swath across daily living. And, when in counseling sessions, we become highly practical by discussing the concrete applications of scriptural principles; what is said is like a two-edged sword that cuts both counselor and counselee.

Moreover, because most of the problems that counselees bring into the counseling room (at bottom) are simply those with which all Christians must grapple, the trainee (and the counselor) is forced to evaluate not only the counselee's life in the light of the Bible's teaching, but his own life as well. It is hard to talk about irregular sleep habits and the scheduling of activities with conviction when one's own life is in shambles in these areas. Again and again the counselor is driven back to God to re-examine his own life, confess his own sins and to make those changes demanded by His Word. So, the counseling session works two ways: not only must the counselor be an example of godliness to the counselee in the biblical-life truths that he emphasizes, but also by the very necessity of emphasizing them, he too finds it continually necessary to re-examine and change his own relationships to God and to his neighbor.

What I am saying is simply this: because the biblical counselor is forced to delve deeply into the meaning of biblical teaching to help

---

[14] *The Christian Couseling & Educational Foundation,* Laverock, Pa. 19118.

his counselee, and because he cannot do so abstractly, but must do so concretely in practical ways, if his basic life set is open toward God and his Word, *this work itself will have a sanctifying effect on him* as well as on the counselee. So, the biblical counselor not only must be a godly man, the complementary fact is true as well — biblical counseling (when done in a truly biblical manner) *will make him more godly.* God's Word sanctifies (John 17:17)!

The tragedy of eclecticism is that the converse is true also: those who spend their time studying, teaching and counseling according to the principles of some pagan system (to the extent that they imbibe these pagan life patterns and commitments) also tend to be influenced by them. A system (like Skinner's) in which man is considered to be nothing more than an animal, and the teachings and practices that one espouses in accord with this pagan evolutionary viewpoint, (in time) tend to divert one's personal life practices. God help Christian counselors who continually subject themselves to such dangers!

The lives of nouthetic counselors, in contrast, continually are challenged, nourished and refreshed by the Word of truth with which they must deal everyday. This is a tremendous plus factor for the counselor himself. It has its dangers of course. Familiarity with the Bible can breed indifference (if not contempt). Yet this is rare (if not impossible) where counseling is truly nouthetic because of the *concrete* nature of what is done. The Word of God is not handled abstractly when it is used nouthetically. When one becomes deeply involved in the joys, the heartaches, the triumphs and the sorrows of a counselee while helping him to relate to God and his neighbor by concrete expressions of love through God's Word, he finds it harder to become cold and abstract. Nouthetic counselors don't talk so much about the counselor's growth in grace; they are too busy working at it!

So, because the system is biblical, it is of the very nature of things that nouthetic counseling itself confronts the nouthetic counselor not only with the constant demand to become godly, but also with the opportunity, structure and requirement to do so. Does any other?

10. Question: Why don't you engage in dialogue with Christian psychologists and psychiatrists?

Answer: Any number of times I have been asked this question; my answer is always the same. I do not do so because I am too busy doing what God has been blessing so greatly. To do so would be to take a side track. I am a pastoral counselor, have taught pastoral counseling for years, and am concerned about pastoral counseling. My prime concerns about psychiatry and psychology, as a result, have to do with their encroachment on the pastor's territory. I want to encourage them to go back to their own backyards.

Now there are at least two ways to do this. I could debate, argue and try to persuade them to do so. That, I am convinced, would in most cases be useless. So, I don't. But the other way I have chosen. By making pastors fully aware of the property given to them in a clear deed from God, I have been trying to persuade pastors to so utilize and cultivate their own backyards that such encroachments from neighbors would become unnecessary and, indeed, highly embarrassing to those who make them.

This approach I believe is succeeding. The self-styled "professionals" (I say *self-styled* because I believe that the Bible teaches that God has called the pastor to be the professional counselor[15]) have felt the impact of thousands of pastors who have themselves begun to take seriously the work to which God called them and for which they are well equipped by their knowledge of the Scriptures. Their writings, disclaimers, concessions, etc. of late give evidence of the fact.

I shall continue to pursue the task of equipping, training, supplying pastors with all the help that I can. That, I believe, is my present call from God. Others, with perhaps a different mission, may want to engage in dialogue with the "professionals." God bless them; but it is not for me.

---

[15]By professional, I mean called to a work as a principal part of his life task.

11. Question: Can a pastor do all of the counseling that you seem to think needs to be done in a local church? Will a pastor have time to do it?

Answer: Yes, a pastor can do all of the counseling he should do in a local church by:

(a) doing biblical counseling which does not take inordinate lengths of time to accomplish;

(b) properly budgeting his time and structuring it according to biblical priorities (see *Shepherding God's Flock,* Vols. I, II);

(c) by eliminating all unnecessary activities from his daily working routine (see *Shepherding God's Flock,* Vols. I, III);

(d) by enlisting elders and deacons and training them to help him in counseling;

(e) by using all of the resources of the members of the flock as supplementary help in counseling (see *Shepherding God's Flock,* Vol. II).

There is always time to do everything that God wants us to do everyday — never one second too few. The only question is what does God want us to do each day?

12. Question: How does your approach differ from Job's comforters' approach?

Answer: It may not be immediately apparent because, for one thing, the Book of Job is not fundamentally a treatise on counseling. There are no principles or directions for counseling spelled out as such. Since the main thrust of the book lies elsewhere, it fails to come to grips with a number of issues that are important to a counselor. But so far as the record does go (and remember that since it is not intended to be a record of counseling technique it is necessarily deficient) there are several differences that are worthy of note.

First, Job's counselors failed to gather data. They came with preconceived opinions into which they tried to fit the situation. It did not fit as the book shows. It is this fact that caused them so much difficulty. Nouthetic counselors, in contrast, are deeply concerned about gathering the facts. The many pages that I devoted to encouraging proper methods of data gathering and to carefully describing the process in the *Manual* provide unquestionable evidence that our approach is quite different from the approach used by Job's counselors.

Secondly, Job's counselors failed to believe him in love. Even when Job countered their charges with protests and arguments to the contrary, they refused to give him the benefit of the doubt. Their minds were made up; facts could not change them. Nouthetic counselors insist upon "believing all things" in love (I Cor. 13:7). That means that it is only the facts that are uncovered by data gathering or in response to homework that can be allowed to drive the counselor to doubt the counselee's word. For a fuller discussion of this point see the answer to Question 13.

Thirdly, Job's counselors failed to focus on the real issue. Job's problem was not that he had brought calamity upon himself because of his sin. Rather, as in many counseling situations, the calamity came through no fault of his own. All of their concern and counsel was wasted in an unproductive insistence upon this point. Because they failed to get the facts and because they failed to listen to Job in love, they became stalled at this point and could not get beyond it. Job's problem was one that nouthetic counselors continually deal with — how to handle suffering for which one is not personally responsible. At first Job handled it reasonably well, but at length, it was at this very point that he broke. Had they met his real need by their counsel, they might have been of significant help to Job. It was about this failure that God, the perfect Counselor, confronted Job in the end.

13. Question: What about love in your counseling?

Answer: I have already said much in my books about love, but let me point out one factor in reply that may add a dimension. Among other things, Paul plainly states that "love...puts up with all things (*stego* means literally 'covers' or passes over), believes all things, hopes all things, endures (or perseveres in) all things" (I Cor. 13:7). Those words provide a clear-cut guide for human relationships everywhere — even in counseling! In contrast to the power of sinful human nature, the Holy Spirit enables the believer to love in such a way that he can avoid taking personal offense, he can give another the benefit of the doubt, he can expect the best of him, and he can maintain these attitudes even when the going gets tough. Without going into each of these qualities in any detail, I should like to observe how important they are in any relationship and then go on to make a point that, in my opinion, is sadly neglected even by biblical counselors.

Tragically, those who seek to inculcate these elements of love in their counselees often fail to demonstrate them by the relationship that they establish in the counseling sessions themselves. I suspect that the reason for this failure lies simply in lack of thought about the application of the practice of love to the counseling context. A moment's reflection will show how vital such an application is. Not only is love necessary for the modeling value that it exhibits and for the establishment of a relationship of trust in which intimate data may be revealed and discussed, but first and foremost the counselor must love his counselee if he seeks to please God. And, biblical counselors know, showing love means more than feeling compassion toward a counselee in his plight; it means doing toward him what God commands.

There are two, and only two, basic relationships between the counselor and counselee, and more often than not these begin to take shape early in the very first session. Once begun, they tend to persist and to harden unless the counselor makes a definite effort to change them. These relationships correspond to two widely differing views of counseling. They always appear in the use of the procedures and the methods appropriate to each view, but are especially prominent in the process of data gathering. The two views of counseling that I have in mind are the biblical view and the non-biblical one. The first is *characterized* by trust, hope and patience; the latter by opposite qualities.

Let us take one aspect of the problem to demonstrate how the two relationships develop and what each produces. According to the non-biblical view, the counselee's description of his problem must be doubted, his word questioned and his motives held suspect. The counselor pictures him either as deceived or deceptive. His problem is to discover which (or how much of which) of these two factors is at work. Consequently, from the outset the counselor refuses to "believe all things," that is to say he refuses to establish a relationship of love. Instead, the relationship begins in distrust and suspicion; hardly the way to begin counseling!

To the contrary, biblical counselors build a trusting relationship of love in which they refuse to doubt the counselee's word. Rather, they make every effort to take what he says at face value.

But what happens when the counselee actually attempts to deceive? What if he has misinterpreted the facts? Does the biblical counselor go on in ignorant bliss? Is the result of Christian love some sort of naivety that makes the counselor gullible to every sort of sinful human perversion of truth? Must the counselor be ineffective because he refuses to discover facts contrary to those at first offered by the counselee? Doesn't such an attitude create insuperable problems for him? No, none of these conclusions follow. Indeed, the opposite of each is true. I Corinthians 13 does not demand that the counselor shut his eyes to facts; it does not teach him to by-pass evidence; nor does it insist that he must ignore the realities of sin. The key difference in the two approaches is not that one tries to find out the truth and the other simply accepts whatever he is told without question. No, both seek to discover the truth of the matter, but the difference lies in the way in which they go about doing it; that is to say, the difference centers about the relationship that is established in doing so. The biblical counselor understands that God insists that facts, not suspicion, must drive him to question another. That is different from entering into the relationship with a chip-on-the-shoulder attitude. And, since the nouthetic counselor emphasizes biblical change and gives weekly homework assignments, it will not be long before the facts that show distortion or deception — if they exist — will be forthcoming.[16] Using a biblically unified system out of a sincere desire to help the counselee by demanding biblical change in the name of God, he expects that any such information will emerge in short order. And in love, the counselor will make every legitimate attempt to put the best construction upon these facts when they do emerge; he will "hope all things." Moreover, when adequate probing or failure to complete homework bring distortion or deception to light, the counselor will not give up. In love he will then deal with this, too; he will "persevere in *all* things" (even in this).

Probing, likewise, may be done in two attitudes, with two objectives in view. Probing for facts may stem from love, from the desire to learn all of the pertinent data in order to help the counselee in the best way possible. When this is the attitude/objective of the counselor, the counselee will know it; he will communicate it to him. In short, the biblical counselor must be *driven* to suspect and question by facts alone. On the other hand, the probing that grows from unloving suspicion seeks to discover discrepancies. You can be sure that the counselee detects this, too. Frequently, the sort of needed information later communicated by the counselee depends upon which of these stances he has discovered in the counselor. ("If he didn't believe what I said before, why should I think he'll believe this either?")

The biblical approach puts the counselor on the right basis with the counselee from the outset. When he continues to show love throughout the sessions that ensue, he will maintain the proper relationship. Not only is the right attitude for building a trusting relationship enhanced by love, but (interestingly) biblical counselors often find that such love has the power to encourage the very thing that it seeks (just as the power of distrust often produces what it suspects). The Spirit of God, who inspired I Corinthians 13, will give Christian counselors the strength to cover, to believe, to hope and to endure. It is by such love, in part, that he brings about the results desired.

---

[16]Cf. Jay Adams, *The Christian Counselor's Manual* (Presbyterian and Reformed Publishing Company, Nutley: 1973), pp. 298-300; 313-317.

14. Question: What do you do when someone feels inferior?

Answer: What about the person who says "I feel inferior" or "I feel inadequate"? What can be done to help him? Much, but it may be done only by correcting his concept of the problem.

To begin with the counselee must be shown that neither inferiority nor inadequacy are feelings. That is fortunate, because if they were, the solution to the problem would be much more complex than it is. Indeed, it is questionable whether anything at all could be done. You see, that is the reason why many persons who speak about *feeling* inferior or *feeling* inadequate fail to solve the problem. There is no way that they can turn their feelings on and off at will.

But, as I said, the situation demands no such Herculean feat since neither inferiority nor inadequacy is a feeling. Actually inferiority and inadequacy is simply a matter of fact. Individuals *feel* bad because they have judged their attitudes and/or actions to be inferior or inadequate. Notice, they feel bad — ashamed, distressed, guilty, sad, etc. — because they have *judged* themselves to be inferior or inadequate in one or more respects.

A judgment, unlike a feeling, can be investigated to see if it is sound. A sound judgment is one that can be supported by facts. An investigation of the evidence may disclose the fact that the judgment was false, or only partly true. In such cases, the *new* judgment arising out of the investigation will trigger new feelings appropriate to the new evidence.

But, let us say that the facts prove the judgment to be sound in every respect (as in counseling so often will be the case). Then what does one do? First, he should be helped to consider whether it is proper or improper for him to be inferior or inadequate in the particular instance or instances under consideration. Not everyone has gifts for every task. If I were foolish enough to agree to put on gloves and enter the ring with Muhammed Ali, (among other things) I would feel bad as I thought about doing so. Clearly I am inferior and plainly inadequate as a boxer, and indeed I ought to be. So if the facts demonstrate a clear case of inferiority or inadequacy, the counselor's next question must be: "Is this inferiority or inadequacy proper or improper?"

If pride (In some particular is the counselee thinking more highly of himself than he ought to think?), or if failure to make a sober evaluation of one's gifts is at the core of the problem (cf. Rom. 12:3), then the counselor's efforts must be directed toward resolving this difficulty. There are many people in the church of Christ who feel bad because they are attempting to do what they never were and never will be equipped to do. If, for instance, someone does not have the gifts to teach, then he had better learn this as soon as possible for his sake as well as for others. The sooner the better.

But suppose an evaluation of the facts shows that the counselee is inferior or inadequate and need not be. He has the gifts but has failed to recognize or develop or utilize them. In this case the counselor may help him to do so by whatever action is appropriate.

So, if inferiority and inadequacy are viewed as facts about which judgments are made, and about which something can be done, the problem can be met. If they are conceived as feelings, nothing can be done.

Let me visually outline the process of dealing with inferiority.

"I am inferior."
(This is a judgment that may trigger bad feelings.)

An evaluation of the facts may show that the judgment is false. (This will trigger new feelings.)	*An evaluation of the facts* may show that the judgment is true.
But it may be proper to be inferior in this respect. (Right counseling will help the counselee to settle for this and will trigger new feelings.)	It may be wrong to be inferior. (Right counseling will lead to development and use of gifts and this will trigger new feelings.)

15. Question: Why don't you ever speak about people's problems in terms of game theory as many other counselors do?

Answer: My answer to this important question is simply this — I avoid game theory analysis because the Scriptures don't support such an analysis.

Whenever counseling theorists develop game analyses of human problems, they always fail to some extent to take human sin and its tragic effects seriously enough. Sin is no game. Sinning cannot be compared to playing a game. To speak of sin in terms that grow out of game activity, therefore, always minimizes or blunts the edge of the heinous quality of sin as rebellion against a holy God.

It is of the essence of a game that it doesn't count. No matter how seriously one may play or observe a game in the end (everyone knows) the outcome of a game is of no essential consequence. That is why it is a game; not serious life. Of course, money may be lost, jobs may be at stake for participants in sporting contests of various sorts, but these elements are not essential to the game; they are incidental, tacked on. Indeed, it is the peripheral quality of these factors that all the more emphasizes the essential nature of the game as activity that can be ignored in life. Baseball may be played by neighborhood kids on the back lot; it doesn't have to be played by six digit professionals in a multi-million dollar astrodome.

So a game is not a necessary life activity. It is optional. One can go through life and do quite well all the while ignoring golf. He can ignore games in a way that he cannot ignore reality. That is because games are a kind of manufactured or synthetic mock-up of reality. The risks and hurdles in a game are contrived. It is for this reason that when you play a game (without the extraneous monetary or vocational involvements that are not of the essence of the game itself) you can always quit whenever you like; even if you are losing or get tired of playing. You can't do that with life! Life's necessary activities must go on — and you with them — because God won't let you put them aside quite so easily.

So, for these and for many other reasons it is entirely foreign to the biblical spirit of things to analyze and describe a counselee's *life,* with its perplexities, sorrows, sins and failures as games. The game category in such instances is unscriptural.

Let me say quickly that I am not opposing the use of games and activities that are parts of games as analogies of life and biblical truth (cf. Paul's allusions to athletic contests). It is the concept of understanding life patterns by game analysis that creates the problem. To describe and seek to deal with problems and patterns *as games* (not as *similar* or *analagous* to games in one or more respects) is quite a different model. Game analysis and game analogy must be distinguished, not confused.

Of course, the counselee himself may sin by treating life like a game (and that is precisely why a counselor may not). In the course of counseling the counselor may discover that the counselee is handling life or counseling assignments in the semi-cavalier attitude that is expressed in the familiar question "What do you think this is anyway, a game?" Whenever this occurs the counselor not only may, but *must,* speak about his behavior in terms of games. But what he says about the counselee's analysis of life as a game will be negative. How can a game analyst do so? Moreover, how can he speak about sin?

There is nothing wrong about games *per se,* but to speak and act in non-game contexts as if one were playing a game is to fail to take God and the responsibilities that He has imposed seriously. That is serious. When a counselor encourages this by using game analysis as his theoretical counseling construct, it is a colossal mistake.

More and more games may be used as *illustrative* since their use communicates to this generation, but more and more one must be careful even in this because (for many) sports have become the national religion of America.

Christian counselors must avoid the (often appealing[17]) approaches of those who know nothing of the eternal destiny of men. Hell is no game. At the same time, they must continue to take advantage of the many meaningful analogies that games afford.

---

[17]Catchy titles devised by game theorists (like some fishing lures) are more useful for attracting adherents (catching fishermen) than for helping counselees.

16. Question: Why do you use a desk in counseling?

Answer: Incidentally here and there in my writings I have mentioned using a desk in counseling. Since such matters raise questions and concern on the part of some I shall take the time to discuss briefly the rationale behind using a desk (or table).

Questions like "Doesn't it *separate* you from the counselee?" or "Isn't that a barrier to communication?" or "Is this a symbol that the counselor wants protection?" etc. are (in my mind) pointless because they focus upon furniture in a symbolic rather than in a functional manner.

If furniture is employed chiefly for its symbolic effects, those questions might be of significance. But in our counseling it is the functional factor that is uppermost. I use a desk or table *because I need one.*

Since nouthetic counseling involves gathering facts, homework, the use of the Scriptures, etc. many books, papers, pencils, etc. are involved in the process. Frequently, the telephone is put to use in the counseling session. In other words, since nouthetic counselors do more than talk, their work dictates a layout that is a bit more elaborate than that which is required by a counselor who only talks and does no work during sessions.

If, then, the desk or table has a symbolic side, it is simply this — it symbolizes the nouthetic counseling session as a time to *work* on the client's problem. A desk or table is *never a barrier when it is used.* And from the moment, when the Personal Data Inventory is spread out for review, till the final homework assignment that is written, the desk is used in nouthetic counseling.

17. Question: You say a lot about the possible significance of sleep loss. Suppose sleep loss is important. What do I do to get to sleep when I find myself having difficulty doing so?

Answer: This is a very important question. First, before I try to answer that one for you, let me review briefly what I have been saying about sleep loss. The Scriptures are clear that we must not do anything that injures our bodies (cf. I Cor. 6:15, 19). Christians have an additional reason to care for the body. Paul says that the Christian's body is the temple of the Holy Spirit. Therefore, significant sleep loss becomes an issue of importance, if loss of sleep does, in fact, injure the body. Sleep loss studies show that it does (cf. Segal and Luce: *Sleep and Insommia*).

Sleep loss frequently occurs when the counselee has an unresolved problem that he has failed to commit to God. In this way it becomes an additional or complicating problem, that has more serious immediate effects than the original problem. Yet, though sleep loss in some persons may lead to effects similar to those experienced by ingesting LSD, these effects can be eliminated by getting sleep. So it is important to know how to tell the counselee to find sleep when it tends to elude him. The following factors may be advised:

1. Put your unsolved problems in God's hands before going to bed; don't carry them to bed with you. Solve all problems with others before going to bed; "Don't let the sun go down on your anger."

2. Keep a pencil and pile of index cards next to your bed on which to jot down thoughts that occur that you don't want to lose overnight. Resolve to make these brief one-line notes. (Limit yourself to only one index card per night.) Don't turn your night notes into writing sessions.

3. Begin to keep regular habits. Get up and go to bed at the same time almost every night. Your body will adjust and grow tired just at the right time in a short while.

4. Exercise (see your doctor if there is any question about doing strenuous exercises), through hard work during the day and perspiring exercises not long before retiring, may help.

5. Stay in bed. Most people who have trouble sleeping get up. This

is a mistake. Don't eat, read, watch TV, etc. when you ought to be sleeping. Go to bed and stay there. Allow yourself to think about nothing else but going to sleep. Sound boring? Good; boring enough to put you sleep!

6. Drink some milk before retiring. There is some evidence that milk contains chemical elements that may help you to sleep.

7. Don't take sleeping pills. They often bring about a type of sleep that is deficient in R.E.M. (rapid eye movement) stage sleep (the kind especially required by persons who have experienced sleep loss).

8. Be sure to do a satisfyingly hard day's work (read Eccl. 5:12).

9. Sometimes a relaxing hot shower before retiring helps.

10. Sexual relations leading to orgasm (in marriage) help.

All or some of these factors will apply to each counselee who is having sleep problems. Often counselees need instruction and suggestions. Persons who have followed these carefully report that their sleep problems evaporate quickly.

18. Question: What does the word nouthetic mean?

Answer: After all that I have written about this matter I am still asked this question rather frequently. Let me give a succinct reply that I trust will answer this once and for all.

Nouthetic is a word that I brought into English from the Greek New Testament to describe the biblical emphases in counseling that have been distorted or missed for so long. It stresses three things (all three elements are in the word):

1. The counselee has a problem that must be resolved.

2. This problem must be resolved by verbal confrontation.

3. The resolution must be done for the benefit of the counselee.

The word, used in a Christian setting such as the New Testament, looks more like the following:

1. The counselee has problems resulting from sin that must be resolved God's way.

2. These problems must be resolved by verbal confrontation using the Scriptures.

3. The resolution must be done out of love for the counselee to help him love God and enjoy Him in his life.

19. Question: How do you counsel unsaved persons?

Answer: In one form or another this question always arises in a discussion or in a question-and-answer session. Many people are perplexed about this important matter, and it deserves more adequate attention than I can give to it here. I hope (D. V.) in time to write a book on the subject. My response here will be preliminary and minimal.

To begin with, any counseling worthy of the name Christian must include a place for evangelism. If the system by which one counsels excludes evangelism (as do all secular systems of necessity), this in itself is an adequate indictment of that system. Can you imagine the apostle Paul engaged in giving counsel to an unbeliever that did not include a presentation of the gospel of Christ? Can you imagine him trying to mend a broken marriage without referring to the biblical priorities pictured most fully in the relation of Christ to His bride the Church, for whom He died? Can you imagine him calling hopeless and helpless unbelievers to Christian living when they have neither biblical insight nor spiritual (spirit-given) power to engage in such living?

The answer, then, to the question is simply this: we evangelize unbelievers as did the Lord and His apostles. To do otherwise would give false hope, false security and misdirection. To do otherwise would dishonor God, show unconcern for the unbeliever, and lead to ultimate failure. Adequate solutions to life's problems can be found nowhere but in Jesus Christ. To not point to Him by presenting the good news is to point elsewhere. If the "fruit of the Spirit" is the goal of counseling, then counseling that ignores the regenerating, illuminating and enabling work of the Spirit is futile.

Presenting the gospel to an unbeliever in counseling is not significantly different from presenting the gospel to an unbeliever in some other setting. All of the accepted biblical principles of evangelism apply. There is one advantage, however. In God's providence, when an unbeliever comes to a Christian counselor for help he thereby:

1. Admits by that very act that he does not have the answer to his problem. The framework for a gospel presentation, therefore, will be something like this:

a. You admit that you don't have the answer to your problem.

b. That is because you haven't considered God's answer.

c. But His answer is larger than what you've asked for. In meeting the problem that you've asked about He always first meets a more basic one — your relationship to Him. What He says is that there is a basic reason why you don't know His answer — you don't know Him.

2. Admits that he is at least interested in considering a Christian solution to his problem (if he knowingly seeks a *Christian* counselor). How tragic when a Christian counselor disappoints him by not meeting his expectations for a distinctively Christian answer. If the unbeliever seeks help from a Christian counselor, not realizing that he is a Christian, the counselor may still make a point of the fact. "In God's providence," he may say, "you are going to get more than you expected."

Of course, in approaching the unbeliever with a gospel presentation, the counselor must use wisdom. He must either sense that conditions are proper for presenting Christ's claims or do what he can minimally to clear the way for such a presentation. By clear, proper conditions I mean such things as an ability to listen (a drugged or drunken person is not in condition to hear the message; nor is a person who is afraid that his wife will leave him on the next train out of town). Minimally, the counselor may need to offer other help first (like extracting a promise from the wife to stay and enter into counseling). Before the counselee is in a state in which he can even consider the message it is useless to attempt to present it.

Then, too, the approach will differ with each person and with each situation. Jesus evangelized Nicodemus immediately upon the opening of their conversation. In the next chapter (John 4) He worked more gradually with the woman at the well. (He spoke of water and buckets and ropes and hills and husbands. She saw Him as a teacher, then a prophet and only at last as the Messiah.) In John 9, He healed the blind man and left. He did no evangelizing on that first encounter. The blind man had nothing more to say than "I know only this one thing — once I was blind but now I can see." On a second encounter He spoke to him about the need for healing the blindness of heart. Two facts emerge: Christ always pressed the claims of the gospel soon upon everyone. But, also, He used a sense of timing in doing so. He often did some other thing, for the person who was in need of the gospel, first. Then, through that He reached him with the message of salvation.

The Christian counselor must recognize that it is fruitless to offer anything other than minimal help before evangelizing; apart from the resources of the Word and the Spirit all counseling is superficial. And, the Christian will settle for nothing less than *depth* counseling; he believes in change brought about by *God*. Yet, to clear the way for a presentation of the way of salvation, he recognizes the importance of doing something else first.

What he does must be done biblically, and it must be done sincerely (out of concern for the counselee; not *merely* to clear the way for evangelism). What he does must never be a gimmick. So the Christian counselor's approach frequently (perhaps *most* frequently) must be two-handed: in the one offering immediate help in the situation, while holding the Word of life in readiness in the other. He will bring forward his second hand as soon as possible.

The reason I have not spoken often about evangelism in counseling (but see one early article in *The Big Umbrella* on the subject) is because (1) biblical counseling of any depth must begin at salvation (everything before is in one sense pre-counsel). You can't have true sanctification apart from the Spirit; (2) the pastoral counseling need is so great in the church today and it takes precedence over all other counseling for the pastor (for whom I have written principally).

20. Question: How long does it take to become an effective nouthetic counselor?

Answer: This question is difficult to answer because any given counselor's knowledge, skills and commitment may differ greatly from another's when he undertakes the task of becoming a nouthetic counselor. Moreover, if he is filled with counseling ideas of a non-biblical sort, the laundering process may take some time before much progress can be made. Again, circumstances will make a difference. If one counselor has fifty cases in twelve months and another has but fifteen, all other things being equal, the first has a much greater opportunity for growth than the second.

So, all that I am about to say must be very general and in particular situations may prove to be far-off the mark. Nevertheless, as a bench mark, let me make a stab at answering.

Experience over ten years in training hundreds of pastors leads me to say that the average minister must counsel regularly (4-6 cases per week) for about a period of twelve months, while actively reading, evaluating and improving what he does to become comfortable in his role as a nouthetic counselor. Of course, this is a gross generalization; it may have as many exceptions as not. Ministers differ in gifts and backgrounds as well as opportunities. When I suggest twelve months I speak about a man with good (not exceptional) basic gifts for ministry who is *beginning* to do nouthetic counseling. And I have in mind someone who is studying and learning on his own.

If a minister can sit-in on the counseling of another, watching and participating as a part of the counseling team, he can learn much more rapidly. The discipleship process just described, perhaps, can cut the period in half. Such training is available at C.C.E.F., but also may be acquired by ministers who are already trained to sit-in on their counseling sessions.

21. Question: Have you done research on the results of nouthetic counseling?

Answer: No. And I am not sure that such research, if done, would reveal much that is accurate, useful or helpful. We are not dealing only with quantifiable entities. When someone grows by grace how can that be measured? *Should* it be measured? Is the fruit of the Spirit measurable? In other words, is it possible to research the Spirit of God? Plainly His results are ascertainable like the effects of the wind but their extent, the motives behind them, etc. are hardly quantifiable. Is sanctification altogether removed from mystery? The work of God cannot be analyzed definitively except by divine revelation itself. Yet, even that revelation contains an element that goes beyond human evaluation.

Nouthetic counseling probably can be compared and contrasted statistically with other systems at some superficial points, but these comparisons must be inadequate. Since it deals with the divine it stands in a class by itself. Its uniqueness is that it is not a purely human process. Therefore, even at this point, its method and its evaluation must differ. To agree to the same sort of evaluation as other systems is to abandon the fundamental stance on the Word and Spirit. When all is said and done, each nouthetic counselor knows that his counseling, and how faithful it was to God and His Word, can be evaluated by God alone. It is enough that in His time He will do so.

22. Question: Why can't you use the methods of other counseling systems?

Answer: This frequently asked question deserves an answer. And the answer that I give may help you to understand my position better; at least I certainly hope so.

First, let me point out the obvious fact that well-thought-through systems are self-contained packages. Freud refused to use Jung's methods; Skinner refuses to use Rogers' methods; and Rogers refuses to use Skinner's. Why? Because each of these men had a clear conception of what he thought man's problem was and what the solution to it was when he developed his methodology. Therefore, he drew straight lines from problem to solution when he developed his methods. Methods that would take a route all-around-Robin's-barn, or that would lead away from the target solution were rejected. Many eclectic Christians have not yet recognized this simple fact. Instead, they go on using methods from pagan systems, designed to reach pagan goals, that they hope will lead to Christian theistic objectives.

"But," you object, "can't Christians learn about listening from Rogers or about talking from Freud?" Here is where confusion arises. All counseling uses talking and listening (even Christian counseling) but (*let me make this explicit*) that is quite a different thing from using *Rogerian* listening or *Freudian* talking.

"Why?" you ask. "How does it differ?" Perhaps if you distinguish between *methods* and *means* (as I do) you can see the difference. It may be, of course, that other terms might be more accurate or more useful, but the distinction between these two concepts must be made — whatever labels you gum on them. (Don't get hung up over the words: just learn to distinguish.)

A *means,* as I see it, is a non-oriented entity (so far as a system is concerned). It is a bit of action (like note-taking) or a bit of information (like sleep loss causes hallucinations in some persons). Means may be abstract concept tools—things (he has the *means* to buy it), activities like praying, reading the Word (*means* of grace). There may be many ways and means.

A *method,* as I use the word here, is oriented and systematized. It is goal oriented and consists of structured ways of using means. It is, so to speak, a method *for*. That is to say it is a method for accomplishing some desired end or goal (as in Christensen's method for playing the jazz piano; or the Palmer method for learning penmanship).

Compare and contrast the following in the light of this important distinction:

Means	**Methods**
1. Talking	1. Ventilation — talking for tension release.
2. Listening	2. Rogerian listening — listening for feelings only.
3. Reward/Punishment	3. Skinnerian S/R view — reward/aversive control for animal training.
4. Acting	4. Psychodrama — for inducting inner change in the actor.
5. Questioning	5. Socratic Method for obtaining agreement by supplying direction and answers through leading questions.
6. Scripture	6. Flip-and-point method for discovering God's will.

These six samples of the distinction should show clearly that while a Christian can use all six means, he may not use any of the six methods. Against them he would find it necessary to develop six methods for the use of these means that accord with biblical presuppositions and principles. So, for instance, he would use an expositional/telic method (see *The Use of the Scriptures in Counseling*) rather than the flip-and-point method. That would be an important difference to a pastor, and he would be quite upset if someone charged him with using the flip-and-point method *because he used Scripture.* The two methods of scriptural use cannot be identified; they are entirely distinct. The one is magical; the other is not. The one makes use of context, historical and exegetical work, etc.; while the other refuses to do so.

Pastors can readily see the difference between the two methods of scriptural use. Can they also see that to use talking in counseling is not necessarily the same as using the talking-method called ventilation; or to use listening (for data gathering, for instance) is not the same as to use it for Carl Roger's concerns in his way; or to acting out a conversation as a rehearsal that a husband must carry on with his wife in order to seek her forgiveness, is not the same as Moreno's psychodramatic method for inducing change in the actor?

So when someone asks me, "Can't we use the Rogerian reflecting method for...?" I point out that this is a methodological question (note the telic or purpose element in the words method *for* . . ."), and that methods do not stand alone but are parts of systems. If they are speaking of using the *means* of replying or answering, I would have no trouble in saying, "Of course we reply to and answer the questions of counselees." But replying or answering are means that are used in quite a distinctive way when they take the form of reflective Rogerian replies and answers. And to that, I would have to reply "no," because reflection is *a method* that Carl Rogers uses *for* evoking the supposed pre-packaged solutions to human problems from within the essentially good inner core of the counselee. He designed this method because he wanted the man to be autonomous of others — God, the church, etc.

Whenever one asks the question, "Can we use...?" the answer should be possibly "but *for what?*" That moves between the method and the means to give us an answer at both levels. All sorts of means are useful and valid for Christian counselors; but only biblical methods may be employed.

23. Question: What is conscience?

Answer: It is not a sort of prepackaged box with which each man comes equipped from the creative hand of God. Conscience is not information, a value system, etc. Rather, it is the capacity that a human being has to make self-evaluations (Rom. 2:15) and to trigger the appropriate bodily responses to these that warn us of the guilt of violating our value systems or declare our innocence. The conscience must be informed more and more by Scripture for one to have an adequate standard by which to make satisfactory evaluations of his own attitudes and actions.

Literally the Greek word for conscience (*suneidesis*) means "a knowing together." Thus there emerges in the heart of this concept the idea of *self-* evaluation. There is no moral, self-evaluation going on in a cat.

There are three aspects to the conscience: (1) prosecutor and defense attorney, (2) jury, (3) judge who pronounces sentence and punishment (for more on this, see the *Manual,* p. 94).

The conscience is not our guide; the Scriptures must be that. Conscience may be weak, and ill-informed. And it may be "seared" or made ineffective by failure to heed it. Thus a better standard is needed.

Yet, conscience, because of its ability to produce negative emotional warning signals is a valuable capacity with which the counselor must align himself rather than try to water it down and weaken it as the Freudian psychotherapist attempts to do.

24. Question: How is it in the history of the world that we are just now discovering all about nouthetic counseling?

Answer: The answer is that we are not. While it is true that our generation inherited a situation in which psychology and psychiatry had taken over much of the counseling work that originally belonged to and was done by pastors, that situation is unique in the history of the New Testament Church.

The "cure (or care) of souls" is as old as the Christian Church. Psychological and psychiatric counseling is the new and innovative thing. At one time, not too long ago, it was pastors who wrote books on melancholy (the modern word for this is depression). It was men like Ichabod Spencer who did counseling and wrote-up counseling cases for the instruction and help of other pastoral counselors (see *Spencer's Sketches,* Vols. I, II).

No, nouthetic counseling is not new. What is new is the systematic approach to biblical counseling and instructing others. Until now, what was done in all areas of practical theology (preaching and pastoral work included) was done unsystematically. Such work in preaching is still in its infancy and pastoral work itself has hardly been touched in any systematic way.

It is my concern to see all of the practical areas of the ministry developed in a more practical form with a solid biblical and theological base, but not stopping with that, or merely skipping-over methodology to exhortation. The how-to must be developed; otherwise, the principles can be taught only abstractly, not in a way in which they can be incorporated into ministry.

The unique feature of nouthetic counseling has been the concern to be biblical, theological *and* practical.

25. Question: How do you counsel husbands and wives when only one will come?

Answer: I have discussed this elsewhere, so I shall only outline the main features to remember and add (in a bit more depth) one or two new elements.

1. Keep it in mind that the Bible does not allow you to talk negatively about the absent party. Tell the wife/husband who is present to go home and inform the absent party that you refused to do so. Ask the counselee to tell the absent party that you talked only about his/her problems and have him/her show the absent party that his/her assignments all pertain to him/her.

2. If the absent party is a member of the church, the pastor can take the initiative to see him/her by requesting him/her to come next time. In rare instances, if there is sustained refusal to work out matters with the other party church discipline may be required to bring it about (Matt. 18).

3. Assuming that the party who has not come is an unbeliever, over whom the church has no direct care and can exercise no discipline, what can be done? Here are some things:

a. Work on the life of the party who is present.

b. Get the counselee to make a list of his/her failures as a person, as a husband/wife, and as a father/mother. Ask the absent party to look it over, add or modify, etc.

c. Send back thanks for the absent party's help.

d. Ask the absent party to help the counselee in various ways to effect the commitments he/she has made by checking up, reminding, etc.

e. At some point write a note, send a tape recording, phone or visit the absent party to urge his/her presence for a crucial session so that what the original counselee is about to do may be heard and understood more fully by him/her. In this way he/she will be less likely to hinder progress unwittingly. This should occur after evident change in the counselee has been made.

In such ways, often you can help counselees to get absent parties to come for counseling after all. This gradual method of involving the absent party from afar does not always succeed, of course, but in our experience at the center, if he/she is involved in truly legitimate assistance tasks to help the counselee to make significant life changes, it *often* does. Frequently after four to six sessions the absent party appears along with the counselee. He/she comes because he has become interested and is appreciative of (1) what has been done for the counselee, (2) being kept informed, (3) being included in the helping process and (4) a clear-cut refusal to talk about him/her behind his/her back.

4. Remember, your concern is to deal with the person present; not to discuss the sins and failures of the one who is absent. "But how can I talk about my problems in dealing with my husband without talking about all the wrong things that he has been doing to me?" a wife may ask. I answer by drawing a hypothetical picture of what a husband might be like. I paint the worst picture imaginable — till she says "Well, it's not quite that bad." Then I say "I'll show you how God can help you to respond to a man like that in a righteous way. If you can do that, you can respond to your husband too."

I wrote the following to supply some answers to questions raised about nouthetic counseling. They are rather typical, so that this Reply provides a sort of summary that may be helpful.

A Reply to a Response[18]

In Volume I, No. 8, 9 of the *Counselor's Notebook,* there appears a review and response to my *Christian Counselor's Manual.* Since I have been invited to write a reply, I shall do so briefly, pointing out some of the areas in which I think that the reader may be misled by the review and response, with the hope of clarifying any such issues.

First, let me thank Mr. David E. Carlson for taking the time to read and review my materials, and for considering them worth the effort. I appreciate the spirit of his review and response and plan to reply in a similar one. His "encouragement" to be "critical and reflective" about his thoughts is welcomed.

Let me say about Vol. 1, No. 8, p. 1, that there is no less

---

[18]Appears here with little alteration. I have included this because it covers many areas briefly.

"brashness" in the *Manual* than in *Competent to Counsel.* The audiences and the situation differed in writing each. The first volume was aimed at awakening a sleepy church to the dangers all about; the second was written for those who thus were awakened and wanted more of the sort of positive material that also was offered in *Competent.* That I have not relented in my concern, my more recent booklet, *Your Place In The Counseling Revolution* should make clear. Often "brashness," clarity and conviction are confused. Simplicity and simplistic also are words too easily exchanged.

That there is an advance (not a contradiction) in the *Manual* over *Competent* is true. Other books (e.g., *Shepherding God's Flock, Vol. II.* and *The Use of the Scriptures in Counseling*) have additional advances. Any growing movement will show similar filling out.

Comments about *nouthetic confrontation* are somewhat misleading. The emphasis of the Scriptures is upon what God says, not what man says. But any notion that listening (of a biblical — not of a Rogerian sort) is unimportant is a false one. In the *Manual* I spent *chapters* on how to gather data (most of which demands careful active listening).

The most serious comment is the one in which Mr. Carlson suggests that all sorts of approaches may be used in counseling. All sorts of *biblical* approaches *should* be used (and nouthetic counselors recognize that these varieties are inherent in *nouthesia*); but not *all sorts of other approaches* are possible (see once more *Your Place in the Counseling Revolution*, on the problem of eclecticism).

On page 2 there is a serious error: Because the *Manual* has a number of chapters that speak of all sorts of preliminary data gathering, etc. I can hardly accept the evaluation that such concerns are "incidental."

I suspect that the reviewer is hung up on the word confrontation, which he views too narrowly and possibly with some negative connotations. Many of his comments appear to stem from a misunderstanding of my idea of confrontation. I use the word almost synonymously with a word like consultation. My term is better though because, like the Greek word, "confrontation" indicates who takes the leadership in counseling.

The matters of failing to discover adequate data about a counselee, and the problem of creating dependency are two of the most carefully and/or fully considered questions in the *Manual*. I challenge the reader to find a fuller treatment of Data Gathering in the writings of any Christian author. And I most emphatically disagree with the implication that I have oversimplified such matters.

As for over-dependency, no system I know of gets people *out on their own* so quickly. I have made it clear that in focusing on homework rather than on the counseling session, nouthetic counselors avoid creating dependency. The reviewer needs to rethink carefully at these points.

As for drawing conclusions from the silence of the Scriptures — nonsense! I have shown in *Competent to Counsel, The Manual, The Big Umbrella,* and *Shepherding God's Flock* that the Scriptures teach: (1) All Christians are obligated to counsel, (2) Counseling — as a life calling — is delegated by God to ordained ministers of the Word. I devote *pages* to this discussion!

It is because I *do* appreciate what the counselee is up against that I offer a biblical *alternative* to his present state. When I devoted so much space in the *Manual* to the importance of offering hope, how could I be charged with lack of such appreciation?

On page 3, I am accused of appropriating all sorts of psychology without knowing it. I deny the charge. I have self-consciously developed every aspect of the system from exegetical work in the Scriptures. That I am familiar with psychological and psychiatric literature does not mean that I have adopted it.

No, I do not use the methodogy of others unless what they do has been borrowed from the Scriptures. Indirectly, and unconsciously, this sometimes happens as psychologists have appropriated value systems or other material from the Judean-Christian culture. Usually such appropriations distort the truth. Much of what appears to be similar, however, in fact is not. (See *many* discussions of this in almost all of my books.)

Is *what* one says less important than *how* he says it, as the reviewer suggests? Perhaps at times; but the statement is generally false if *what* one says comes from the Word of God! I can understand how generally it could be true if one does not. Of course how one presents truth can modify it considerably.

In Vol. 1, No. 9, p. 1, the reviewer misunderstands support — as it usually is conceived. Psychologists frequently *do* encourage support of sinful attitudes and behavior, as I have shown in the *Manual.* To say "It appears you are doing the best you know how. . . " to a counselee, to me is a horrendous statement. How many of us are doing our best even ordinarily, let alone when we get ourselves into all sorts of trouble by our sin? Sinners rarely do the best they know how. Counselees live far beneath their known standards.

The counselor *does* check out what is needed first — else why did I say *so* much about data gathering? The counselee's "readiness to receive help" was fully discussed under questions of agenda and hope. I am once more surprised at the way in which the reviewer asserts that I have not paid attention to matters that I treat at length. Either he has read only superficially or he does not recognize material not stated in his own terminology.

I do appreciate his suggestion to say more about timing. I have said a good bit on this by implication, but little systematically. I shall try to heed his advice.

How the reviewer could ask for more material on the counselee's resistance to change (p. 2) nearly stupefies me. The entire *Manual* was written largely to deal with this issue.

Confrontation does not increase resistance. The contrary is true. People are tired of the other pale help methods and express a genuine encouragement and hope over the fact that at last someone is willing to take the time and trouble to pitch-in-and-help them rather than try to establish relationships, play games or shadow box.

The supposed "dangers" of homework are, themselves, best discovered through homework. Action can never be "premature" if it is appropriate. Some useful efforts always can be recommended, even if they consist of homework designed to elicit more data. Delay of action destroys hope (see the *Manual* for a detailed discussion of this point).

While much more could be said in reply to the review, I offer only these few comments to alert the reader to the fact that the review (in my opinion) is quite misleading. And, may I offer as my most pointed comment, the observation, that in no sense is the review biblical. The reviewer gave his opinions — to which he is entitled — but he did not critique my books according to scriptural criteria. This tendency is the most dangerous of all.

PART THREE

YOUR RELATIONSHIP TO NOUTHETIC COUNSELING

Is this section really necessary? "After all," you may say, "my only relationship to all of this is that of an interested bystander."If that is how you see yourself, then that is *precisely* why the chapter is necessary. Of course, if you are deeply involved in nouthetic counseling already, you will find this chapter important too.

Every Christian is more intimately related to counseling than he may realize. You may never go to a counselor yourself, but the probability is that someone in your family (wife, husband, parent, child, brother, sister) will. Therefore, you should be concerned about the type of counseling that he/she will receive. You may never have done any counseling in your life but — if you are a growing Christian — someone sooner or later is likely to approach you for help. What will you do? How will you help him? Galatians 6:1ff. not only requires you to do so, but even indicates that you should *take the initiative* to help another sinning, suffering Christian whenever God providentially places him in your pathway.[1] In order to do so, you must be prepared. But how can you best prepare for such eventualities?

Furthermore, the church of Jesus Christ, despite the fact that her resources are more abundant and more strategically placed than ever before, is failing to make the impact that she might either in this country or around the world. Why? Doubtless, there are many reasons; but without a doubt one of the major causes of her feebleness lies in the torn, defeated condition of so many individual Christians. Power is leaking out of the thousands of holes with which the church is riddled. These leaks must be plugged if we would

---

[1]For a more detailed exposition of the passage, explanation of your duties and how to perform them, see "You are Your Brother's Counselor," *The Big Umbrella*.

conserve and harness the power provided by Jesus Christ. Unsolved marital struggles, long-standing bitternesses among members of congregations, crippling sinful practices, and the like have so de-energized and demoralized the church that she hardly *begins* to make the impact of which she is capable. Christians, turned inward do not make good witnesses. Christians, licking their own wounds are decidedly unattractive to their unsaved neighbors. The present state of the church, therefore, clearly indicates that the need of the hour is for strengthening, not as an end in itself, but that God's name once more might be honored in the lives of His people. Only then will young and old everywhere come to the Light. They will do so when they see Him shining brightly through the victorious lives of His people. That is the background for evangelism that is needed in these dark and desperate days.

But how will this healing come? Only as those Christians who are concerned everywhere begin to confront one another nouthetically. Personal differences must be resolved; marital and family difficulties must be set to rest; peace between (and within) Christians must become the rule rather than the exception. Massive effort to spread the word about nouthetic counseling, to train as many pastors and other persons as possible in its practice, and to further its aims and principles is now needed. *That* is the strategy of the hour.

If you are a Christian businessman or a housewife who cares, and wonders what you can do, let me make a few suggestions:

First, you can pray. But don't only pray generally. Pray specifically for those who are working in this movement; pray for their families; pray not only for those who think, study and write, but also for every last person who is trying earnestly to learn to counsel biblically. Pray for those whom they counsel. Pray today. Pray that God will send counselees by the droves to them; pray that they will be able to minister to each biblically. Pray for the healing of God's sheep everywhere, that *in our time* the power resident within the church may be loosened in an overwhelming display of grace.

Secondly, you may give. Financially, this movement has been born and raised on a shoestring. Now that vast new opportunities have opened up, support that has never been sought in the past must be obtained for the future in order to solidify many gains, and in order to move in on the opportunities that God has given. These opportunities must not be allowed to slip by.

"But how shall I give?" you may wonder. Support pastors financially so that they will be free to spend adequate time doing the counseling that is necessary. Provide sufficient funds to buy the supplementary literature that they will find useful as handouts when counseling. Pay their way to çonferences, programs, etc. where they can receive more training in biblical counseling. You also may give directly to the Christian Counseling and Educational Foundation through which most of the training is being done and from which much of the literature emanates.[2]

Thirdly, get involved. You have begun to do so by reading this book. There are a number of others available that would help you to see more deeply what nouthetic counseling is all about. A course on cassette tape designed for training laymen to counsel was prepared in the summer of 1974 in conjunction with the Pentagon and for use among laymen in the armed forces. It has been made available to others as well.[3] You may wish to gather a group of interested laymen together for three or four months of weekly meetings to study counseling, using these tapes. Perhaps your pastor would like to use them in conjunction with a prayer group or a Bible study group. Mention them to him. But your involvement will mean more than giving and study; you also must begin to use what you learn. You must begin counseling. Start with those whom God has put in your pathway. Start now.

Fourthly, tell other Christians about your interest and concern. Lend this book to them and then discuss it with them. Invite them to instruction meetings like those suggested above. In every biblically legitimate way try to get others concerned enough to become involved. Be sure, however, that what you are doing among the members of your congregation has your pastor's approval. Be careful that you do not become devisive. You must not allow a counseling clique to develop. Nothing can hurt the work of Christ more than for those who are seeking to heal the church themselves to

---

[2]The address is: The Christian Counseling and Educational Foundation, 1790 E. Willow Grove Ave., Laverock, Pennsylvania, 19118. CCEF is a non-profit corporation so that your gifts are tax-deductible.

[3]Obtainable from Christian Study Services, the bookstore located on the CCEF premises.

become causes of new injuries. Be careful, therefore, and beware of all clandestine activities. Work in harmony and in conjunction with the church.[4] If the pastor and/or elders of the church at first do not agree, be patient. Take time to demonstrate the value of what you have learned by the sort of life that you live in their presence. Help, informally, as every Christian should, wherever God gives an opportunity. By such helpful demonstration, rather than by disruptive tactics, in most instances you will win a sympathetic hearing for the introduction of more formal efforts such as classes, instruction, etc.

Lastly, train someone else. When by God's help you have become a proficient counselor yourself (and here you must make a *sober* evaluation based upon the criteria mentioned in Romans 12:3) invite someone else who is interested, who shows promise and who has studied biblical counseling in some depth to sit in on your counseling as a participant observer (more the observer at first; later becoming more of a participant). Counseling, like swimming or painting, cannot be taught by books and lectures alone; it involves skills that can be learned only by observation, discussion and participation under coaching and critique. In other words, counseling must be taught by the discipleship method.[5] You must disciple others to become counselors.

"But," you may say "I didn't learn how to counsel that way; why do others have to?" Perhaps you (and your counselees) learned the hard way by study, trial, error and correction; is there any good reason for others to suffer too? Moreover, if you became a truly effective counselor the hard way, it was because you were highly motivated to do so; others with less motivation (and perhaps with lesser gifts) will need more help. Moreover, you would have learned more rapidly, better and with far less grief had you too been discipled. In fact it probably would yet be of benefit for you to sit in on the counseling of others. So be ready to give to others the blessings that you were denied.

What then is your relationship to nouthetic counseling? You are a part of it, whether you know it or not. You, your loved ones or

---

[4]If you are in a liberal church where this is not possible, that once more points up the fact that you should reconsider your relationship to such a church.

[5]For more on this see relevant sections in *Competent to Counsel, The Big Umbrella,* and *The Christian Counselor's Manual.*

friends in the next year or so probably will be involved in some form of counseling. As your pastor (or some other Christian leader) counsels you or those close to you, you will want him to do so from a truly biblical stance. Can you do anything *now* to encourage those responsible to assure that, when needed, biblical counseling will be available? Then do it; do it quickly, because the study and the acquisition of counseling knowledge and skills does not come overnight. Six months from now may be too late to begin.

If you, yourself, are ill-informed about Christian counseling (perhaps this book is all that you have read on this subject), quickly become better informed. Consider the following bibliography and begin by reading (in this order) *Competent to Counsel, The Christian Counselor's Manual, The Use of The Scriptures in Counseling, Your Place in the Counseling Revolution,* and *Coping with Counseling Crises.* For the layman's special interest read (at least) excerpts from *The Big Umbrella.* When you have gathered a group together to study counseling, listen to the Pentagon tapes and (at the same time) work your way through the 140 cases in *The Christian Counselor's Casebook.* When you begin counseling, obtain a *Starter Packet* and get some copies of *Christian Living In the Home,* and the *What Do You Do When* pamphlet series to use as handouts in counseling. There are also three larger booklets useful for distribution too. Pastors and elders should read Vol. II of *Shepherding God's Flock.*

"You are certainly anxious to sell your books, aren't you?" you may think. That is not my purpose in suggesting the previous study program. If you can borrow any or all of these books, do so (but you will want your own copy of the *Casebook* since that is a workbook). I have made the foregoing recommendations for study because of the growing number of books that we are making available. I have been asked repeatedly for help in knowing how to begin reading. That is why I have taken the time to outline what I consider the most profitable way in which to do so.

All of the training, the study and the handout materials that are produced from within the nouthetic counseling movement have been designed to help counselors become better counselors by providing instruction in counseling and useful supplements to make his counseling easier and more effective. By His grace, we shall endeavor to continue to do just that. Pray for us, and become a part of us; there is much yet to be done.